Saints of Note

D1416318

Saints of Note

The Comic Collection

Written by **Diana R. Jenkins**

Art by **Patricia Storms**

Pauline

BOOKS & MEDIA

Boston

Library of Congress Cataloging-in-Publication Data

Jenkins, Diana R.
  Saints of note : the comic collection / written by Diana R. Jenkins ; art by Patricia Storms.
      p. cm.
  "Originally appeared in serial form in *My friend: the Catholic magazine for kids* from October 2004 through June 2007."--T.p. verso.
  ISBN 0-8198-7120-6 (pbk.)
  1. Saints--Comic books, strips, etc.--Juvenile literature. I. Storms, Patricia. II. Title.
  PN6728.S226J46 2009
  741.5'973--dc22

                    2008055635

"Saints of Note" originally appeared in serial form in *My Friend: The Catholic Magazine for Kids* from October 2004 through June 2007.

Saints' biographies and supplemental material written by Diane M. Lynch

Design by Mary Joseph Peterson, FSP

Picture Acknowledgements:
Carlo Dolci: p. 51; Congregation of the Sacred Hearts of Jesus and Mary: p. 80; Mary Joseph Peterson, FSP: p. 44; S. Gimignano: p. 33; Tom Kinarney: pp. 75, 92; Virginia Esquinaldo: pp. 68, 87

Published by Pauline Books & Media, 50 Saint Pauls Avenue, Boston, MA 02130-3491

Printed in U.S.A

www.pauline.org

Pauline Books & Media is the publishing house of the Daughters of St. Paul, an international congregation of women religious serving the Church with the communications media.

1 2 3 4 5 6 7 8 9   13 12 11 10 09

Contents

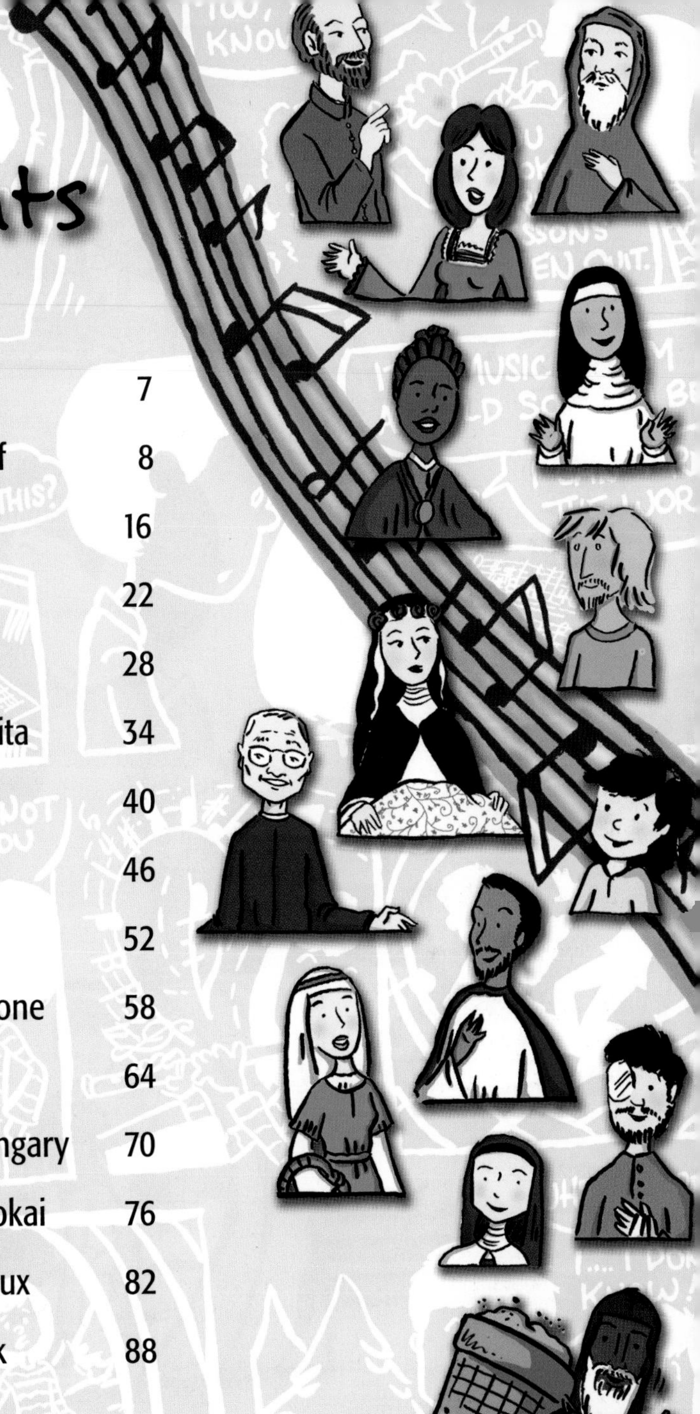

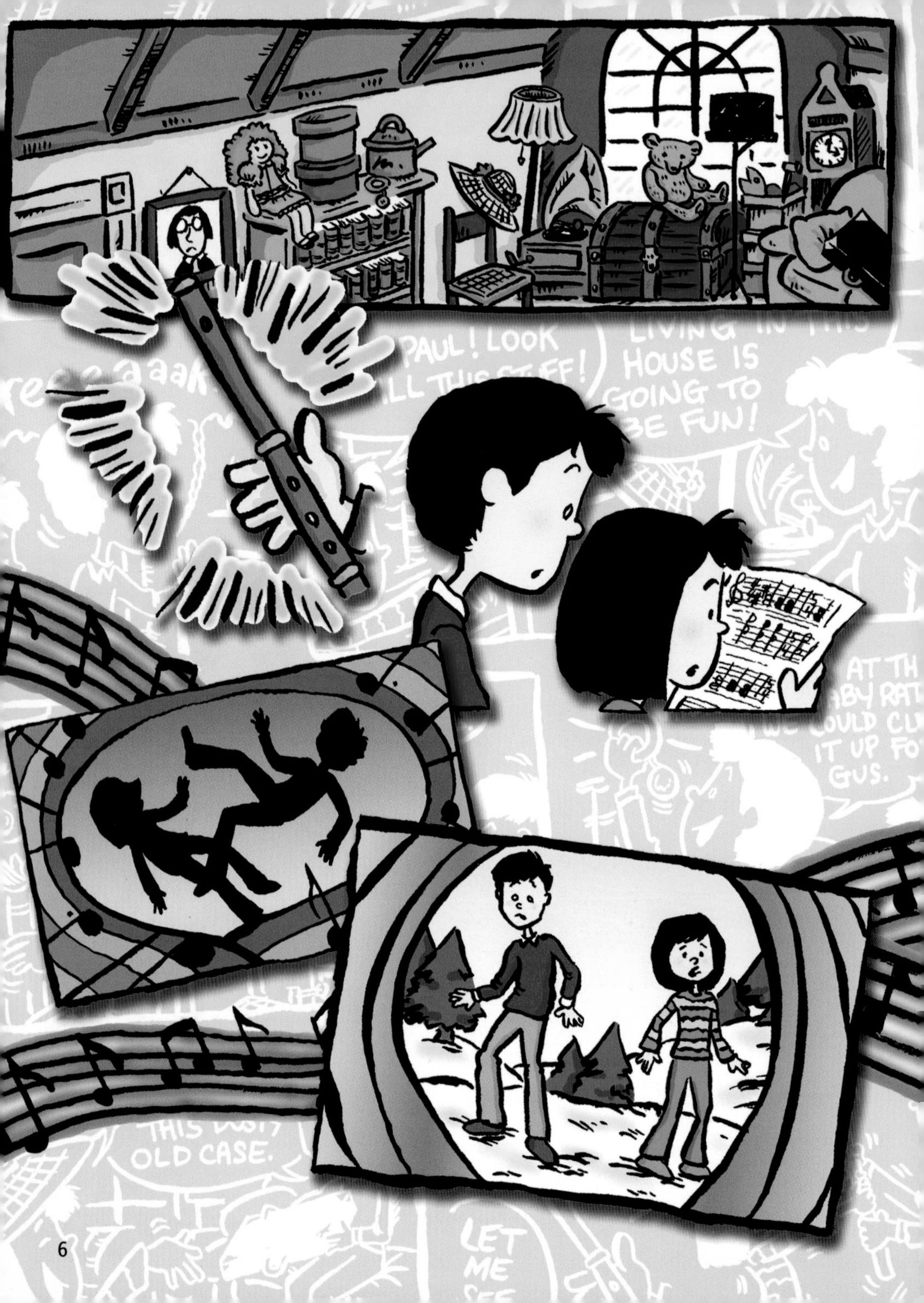
PAUL! LOOK
HOUSE IS
GOING TO
BE FUN!
IT UP FO
GUS.
OLD CASE.
LET
ME

Welcome to Saints of Note!

Many of us look up to athletes, entertainers, and celebrities who excel at a particular talent. Some people earn our admiration by achieving excellence in science, leadership, or other areas. And then there are the saints! We admire these special people because they excelled in loving God and caring about others. This book can help you learn about them.

Cecilia & Paul

Comic strips throughout the book tell the story of the young time-travelers Paul and Cecilia. In each episode, the kids journey to the past, meet a saint, and become inspired to be better people. Their exciting adventures bring the saints to life and make them meaningful for today.

Along with the comics, you'll find detailed biographies, fascinating facts, inspiring quotes, and other useful material to teach you even more about the saints. Sure, it's educational, but it's interesting, too—and it might even help you with homework! (Your teachers will love that!)

I hope you enjoy *Saints of Note*, learn a lot, and get inspired, too!

Diana R. Jenkins

Saint John de Brebeuf

Creeeaaak.....

WOW, PAUL! LOOK AT ALL THIS STUFF!

LIVING IN THIS HOUSE IS GOING TO BE FUN!

I CAN'T WAIT TO READ THESE OLD BOOKS.

BETH WILL LOVE THIS TEDDY BEAR.

HEY, CECILIA! LOOK AT THIS ANTIQUE BABY RATTLE. WE COULD CLEAN IT UP FOR GUS.

OKAY!

LOOK AT THIS HAT!!

I WONDER WHAT'S IN THIS DUSTY OLD CASE.

WHOA! THIS FLUTE MUST BE REALLY OLD.

LET ME SEE IT!

HANDS OFF! LET ME SEE! FINDERS KEEPERS! GIVE IT!

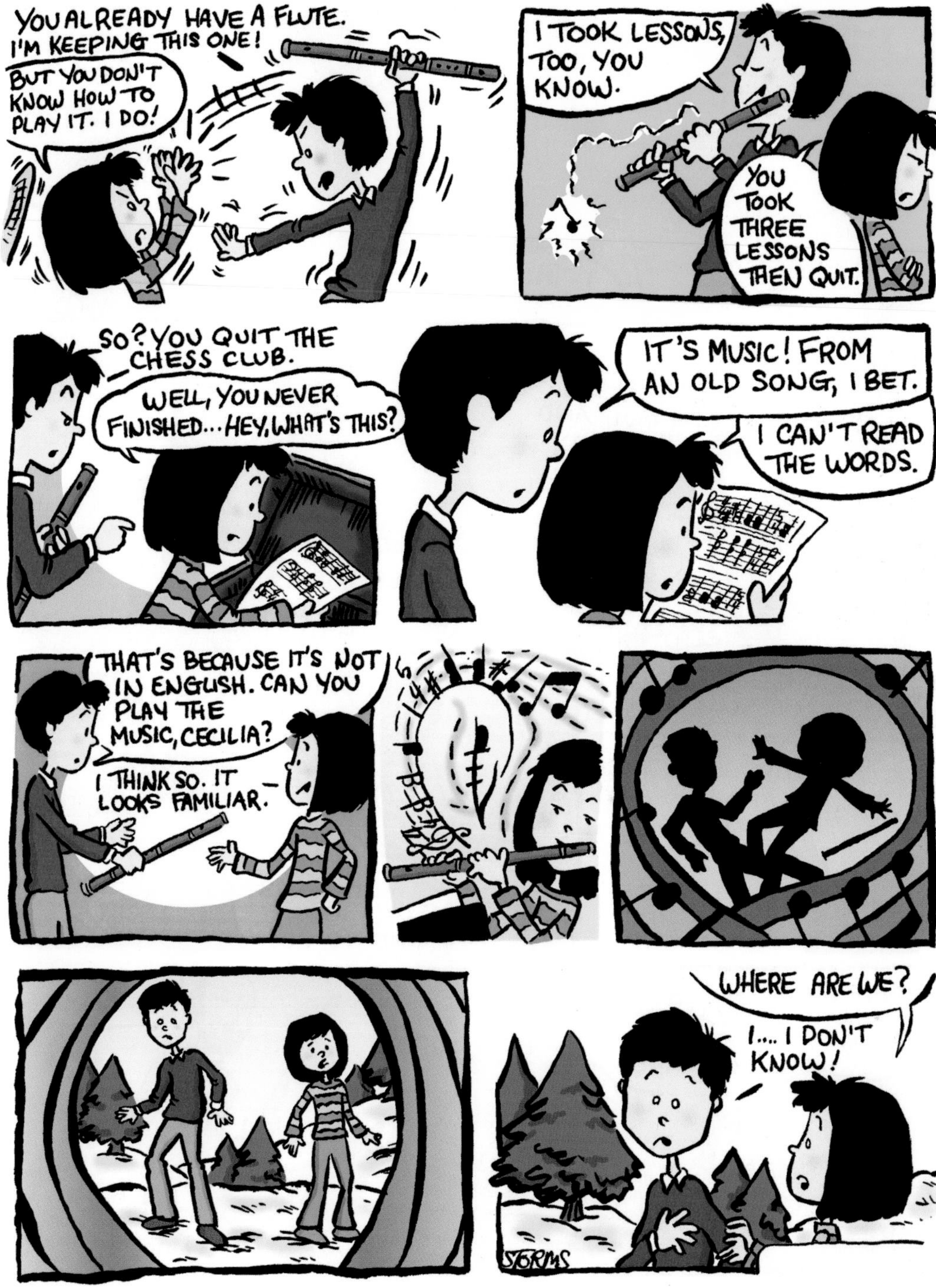
YOU ALREADY HAVE A FLUTE. I'M KEEPING THIS ONE!
BUT YOU DON'T KNOW HOW TO PLAY IT. I DO!
I TOOK LESSONS, TOO, YOU KNOW.
YOU TOOK THREE LESSONS THEN QUIT.
SO? YOU QUIT THE CHESS CLUB.
WELL, YOU NEVER FINISHED... HEY, WHAT'S THIS?
IT'S MUSIC! FROM AN OLD SONG, I BET.
I CAN'T READ THE WORDS.
THAT'S BECAUSE IT'S NOT IN ENGLISH. CAN YOU PLAY THE MUSIC, CECILIA?
I THINK SO. IT LOOKS FAMILIAR.
WHERE ARE WE?
I.... I DON'T KNOW!
STORMS

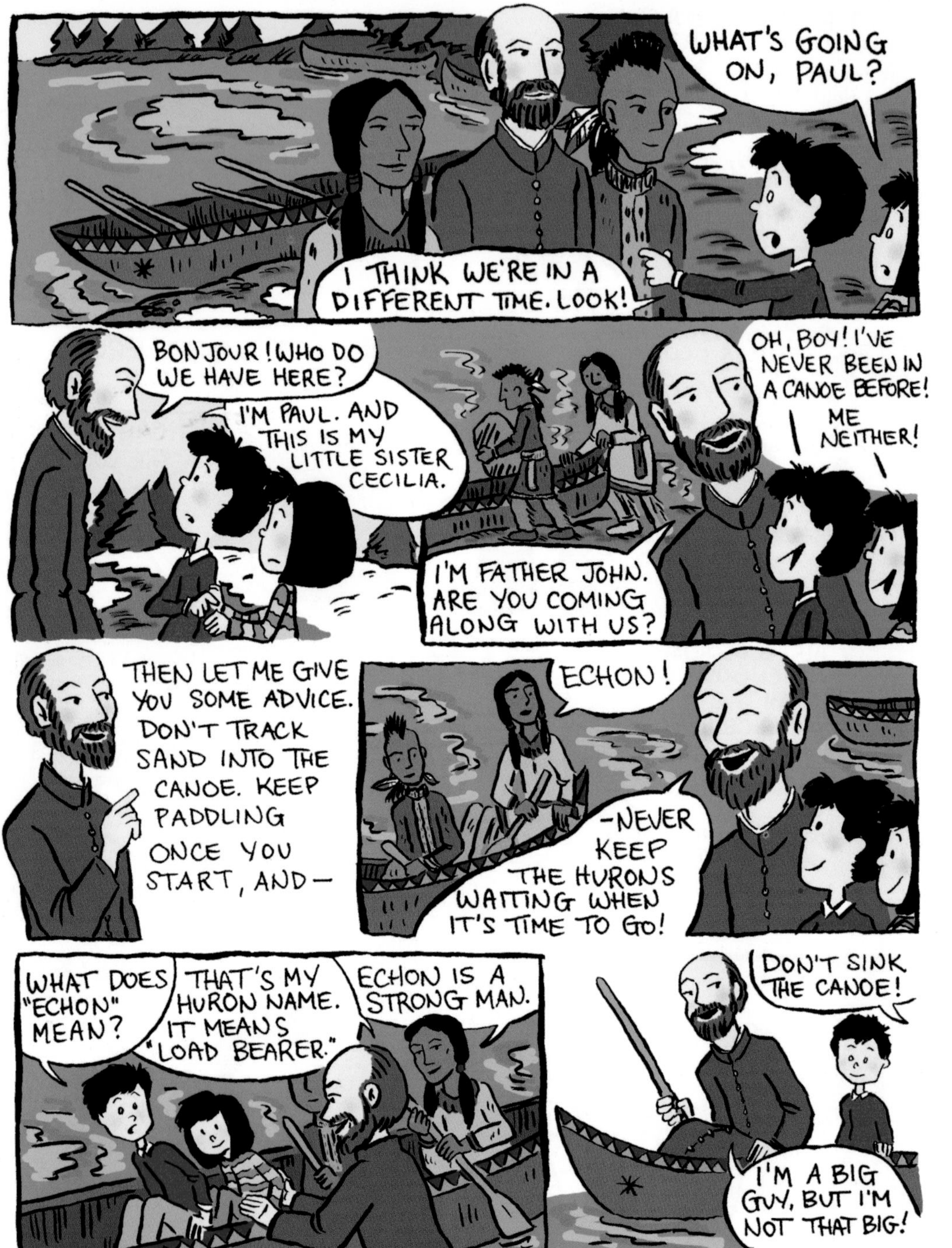
WHAT'S GOING ON, PAUL?
I THINK WE'RE IN A DIFFERENT TIME. LOOK!
BONJOUR! WHO DO WE HAVE HERE?
I'M PAUL. AND THIS IS MY LITTLE SISTER CECILIA.
I'M FATHER JOHN. ARE YOU COMING ALONG WITH US?
OH, BOY! I'VE NEVER BEEN IN A CANOE BEFORE!
ME NEITHER!
THEN LET ME GIVE YOU SOME ADVICE. DON'T TRACK SAND INTO THE CANOE. KEEP PADDLING ONCE YOU START, AND—
ECHON!
—NEVER KEEP THE HURONS WAITING WHEN IT'S TIME TO GO!
WHAT DOES "ECHON" MEAN?
THAT'S MY HURON NAME. IT MEANS "LOAD BEARER."
ECHON IS A STRONG MAN.
DON'T SINK THE CANOE!
I'M A BIG GUY, BUT I'M NOT THAT BIG!

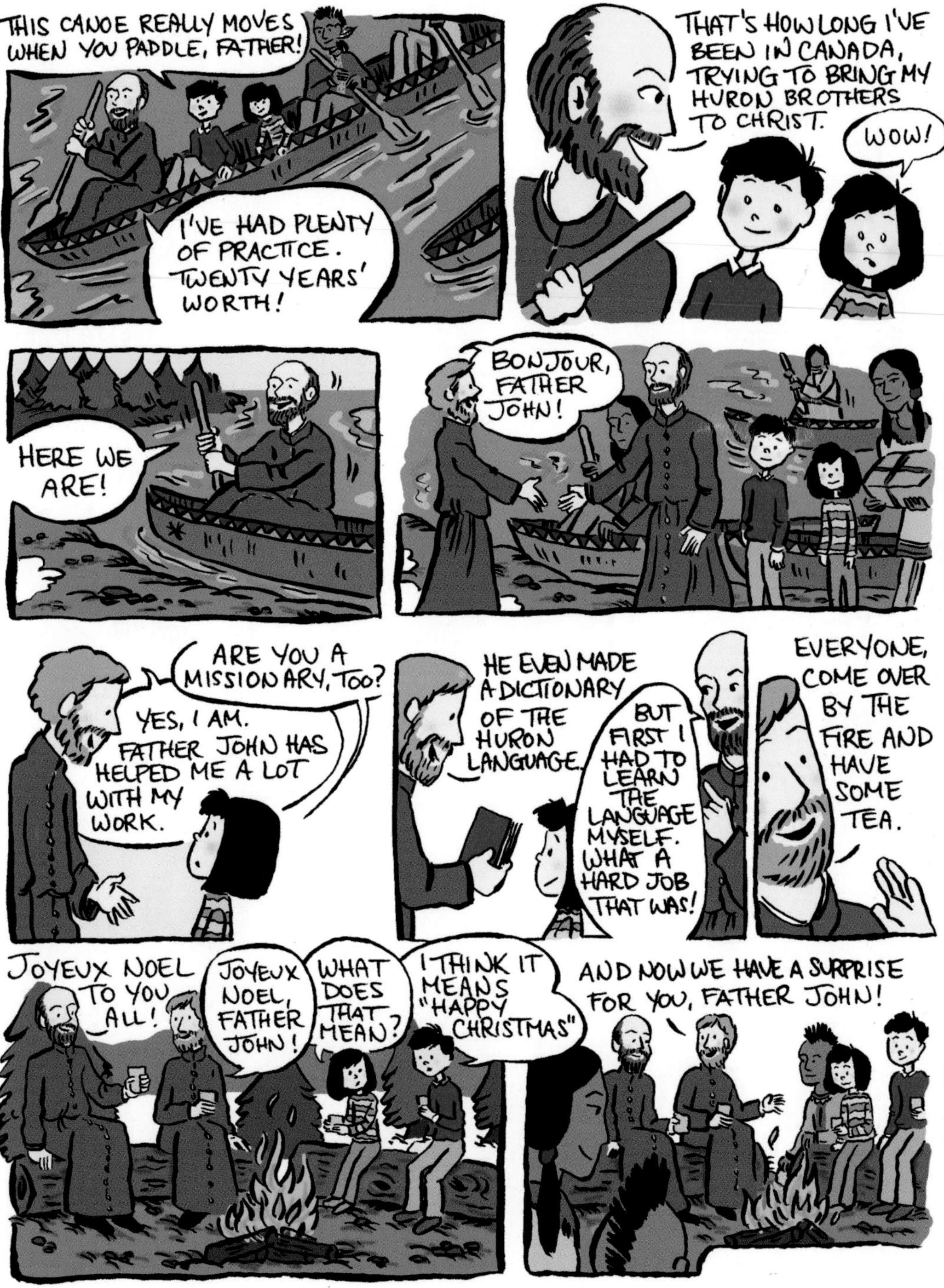
THIS CANOE REALLY MOVES WHEN YOU PADDLE, FATHER!
I'VE HAD PLENTY OF PRACTICE. TWENTY YEARS' WORTH!
THAT'S HOW LONG I'VE BEEN IN CANADA, TRYING TO BRING MY HURON BROTHERS TO CHRIST.
WOW!
HERE WE ARE!
BONJOUR, FATHER JOHN!
ARE YOU A MISSIONARY, TOO?
YES, I AM. FATHER JOHN HAS HELPED ME A LOT WITH MY WORK.
HE EVEN MADE A DICTIONARY OF THE HURON LANGUAGE.
BUT FIRST I HAD TO LEARN THE LANGUAGE MYSELF. WHAT A HARD JOB THAT WAS!
EVERYONE, COME OVER BY THE FIRE AND HAVE SOME TEA.
JOYEUX NOEL TO YOU ALL!
JOYEUX NOEL, FATHER JOHN!
WHAT DOES THAT MEAN?
I THINK IT MEANS "HAPPY CHRISTMAS"
AND NOW WE HAVE A SURPRISE FOR YOU, FATHER JOHN!

ESTENNIA, ON DE TSONWE IESUS AHATONNIA! ONN'AWATEWA D'OKI N'ON, WANDASKWAENTAK!

THAT'S THE SONG YOU PLAYED ON THE FLUTE.

I KNEW I'D HEARD IT BEFORE. IT'S CALLED THE HURON CAROL!

FATHER JOHN WROTE THAT SONG TO TEACH THE HURONS ABOUT JESUS. IT TELLS THE STORY OF CHRISTMAS IN THEIR OWN LANGUAGE.

IESUS AHATONNIA! IESUS AHATONNIA!

JESUS IS BORN! JESUS IS BORN!

THANK YOU, EVERYONE! GOD BLESS YOU, AND JOYEUX NOEL!

JOYEUX NOEL!

HEY, DO YOU HEAR MUSIC PLAYING?

YES! IT SOUNDS LIKE A FLUTE.

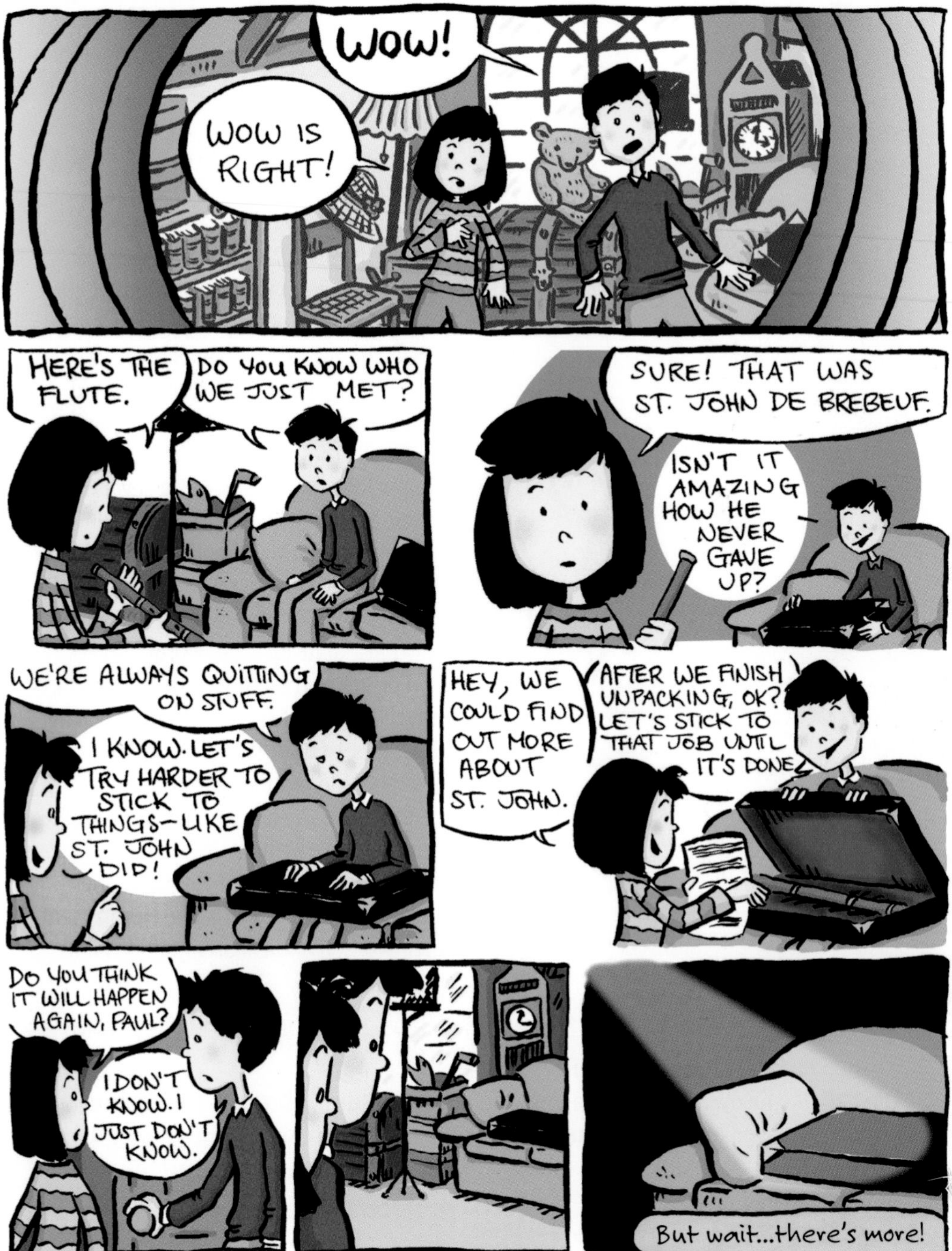
WOW!
WOW IS RIGHT!
HERE'S THE FLUTE.
DO YOU KNOW WHO WE JUST MET?
SURE! THAT WAS ST. JOHN DE BREBEUF.
ISN'T IT AMAZING HOW HE NEVER GAVE UP?
WE'RE ALWAYS QUITTING ON STUFF.
I KNOW. LET'S TRY HARDER TO STICK TO THINGS—LIKE ST. JOHN DID!
HEY, WE COULD FIND OUT MORE ABOUT ST. JOHN.
AFTER WE FINISH UNPACKING, OK? LET'S STICK TO THAT JOB UNTIL IT'S DONE.
DO YOU THINK IT WILL HAPPEN AGAIN, PAUL?
I DON'T KNOW. I JUST DON'T KNOW.
But wait...there's more!

Father John found the Huron language very difficult to learn. "At home you may have been a professor or a theology teacher," he wrote to a friend. "Here you will merely be a student!" However, he kept trying. Eventually he wrote a Huron catechism as well as a French-Huron dictionary for other missionaries to use.

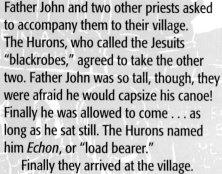

John de Brebeuf was born in 1593 into a wealthy family in France. His love for God and for people led him to enter the Society of Jesus. Soon he met two Franciscans who had just returned from New France (now Canada). After hearing their exciting stories, Father John realized that he too wanted to become a missionary.

In 1625, Father John arrived in Quebec. The following summer, a group of Hurons arrived to trade their furs.

Father John and two other priests asked to accompany them to their village. The Hurons, who called the Jesuits "blackrobes," agreed to take the other two. Father John was so tall, though, they were afraid he would capsize his canoe! Finally he was allowed to come . . . as long as he sat still. The Hurons named him *Echon*, or "load bearer."

Finally they arrived at the village. Father John worked there for several years, but when the English took control, he was sent back to France. At last, in 1633, he was able to return, but it was another year before he could make his way back to his beloved Hurons.

For the next fifteen years, Father John traveled from village to village preaching the Gospel. Outbreaks of smallpox, drought, and crop failures made life difficult. The Hurons were at war with the Iroquois, who in 1649 invaded the village where Father John and Father Gabriel Lalemante were staying. The Hurons sent their women and children to hide in the

Saint John named a game played by the native people *lacrosse*. The stick used reminded him of a *crosier*, or bishop's cross.

Pray for the native people of North America, who have often been misunderstood and mistreated.

PRAYER

Saint John, you traveled to a new land and learned new customs. You never stopped believing in God's love. Help me to love and live his word each day.

PATRON OF CANADA
Feast Day
OCTOBER 19

Saint John de Brebeuf, a tall, rugged man with a gentle heart, was known as "the apostle of the Hurons."

forest, but the Jesuits chose to stay with the men, who were mostly Christians. Soon the Iroquois realized they had captured the famous Echon, the most powerful of the Jesuit blackrobes. The priests, as well as the Hurons, were finally killed. Father John remained faithful to his people and to God until the very end.

Saint John de Brebeuf

15

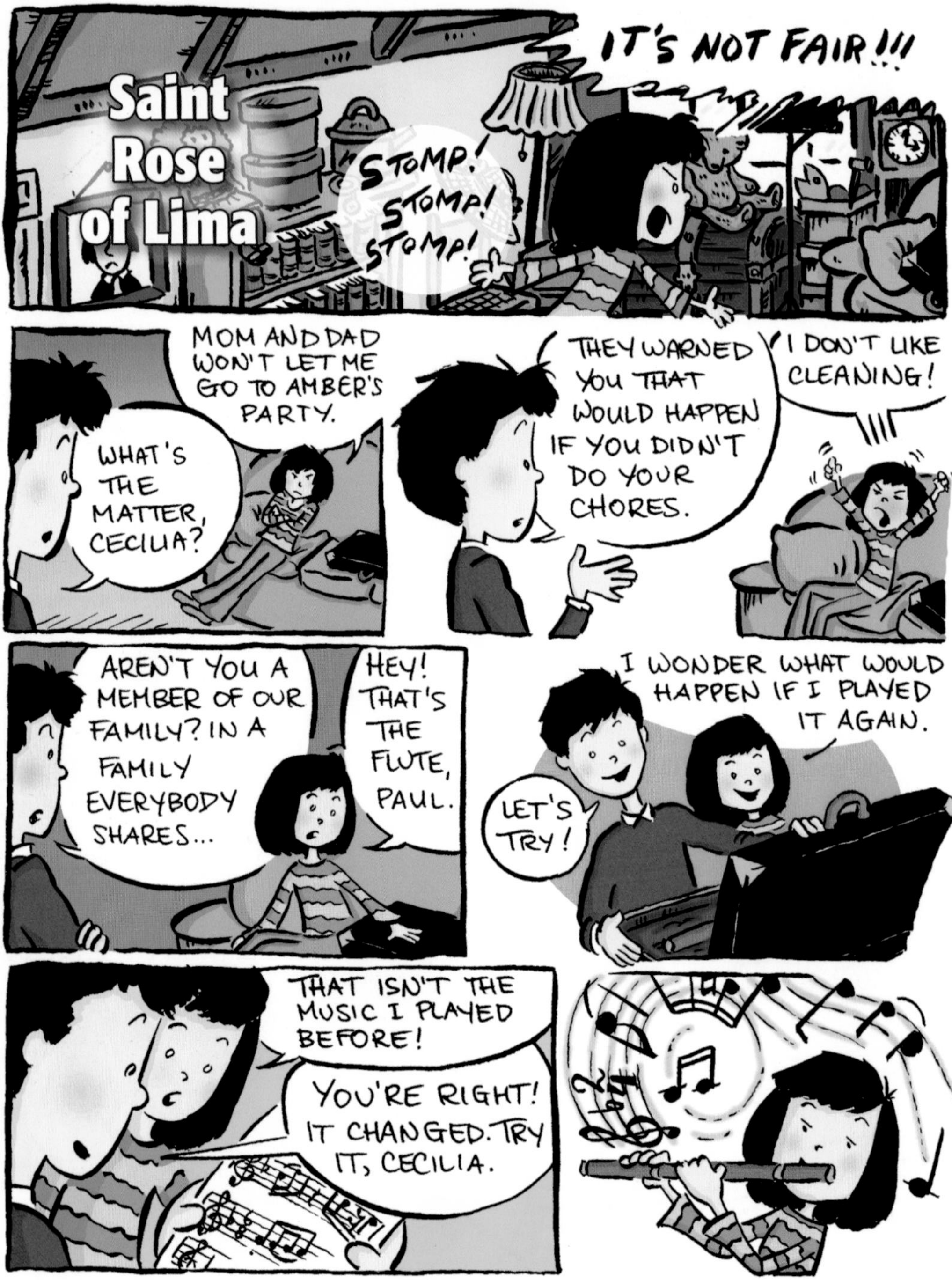
Saint Rose of Lima
IT'S NOT FAIR!!!
STOMP! STOMP! STOMP!
MOM AND DAD WON'T LET ME GO TO AMBER'S PARTY.
WHAT'S THE MATTER, CECILIA?
THEY WARNED YOU THAT WOULD HAPPEN IF YOU DIDN'T DO YOUR CHORES.
I DON'T LIKE CLEANING!
AREN'T YOU A MEMBER OF OUR FAMILY? IN A FAMILY EVERYBODY SHARES...
HEY! THAT'S THE FLUTE, PAUL.
I WONDER WHAT WOULD HAPPEN IF I PLAYED IT AGAIN.
LET'S TRY!
THAT ISN'T THE MUSIC I PLAYED BEFORE!
YOU'RE RIGHT! IT CHANGED. TRY IT, CECILIA.

WHERE ARE WE?

LOOK! THERE'S A LITTLE HUT OVER THERE!

GOOD MORNING, CHILDREN!

WHAT A PRETTY LADY!

HELLO! WHAT ARE YOU DOING?

I'M MAKING A TABLECLOTH. HOPEFULLY, I CAN SELL IT. MY FAMILY NEEDS THE MONEY.

THESE ARE SO BEAUTIFUL!

THANK YOU. I WORK HARD IN THE GARDEN SO I'LL HAVE FLOWERS TO SELL, TOO.

DOES YOUR FAMILY LIVE IN THIS HUT?

NO, OUR HOUSE IS OVER THERE. BUT I LIKE TO COME HERE TO PRAY.

MY FAMILY DOESN'T LIKE IT WHEN I DO THAT. BUT THEN, THEY OFTEN DISAGREE WITH WHAT I DO. IT'S HARD.

I KNOW WHAT YOU MEAN! MY PARENTS AND I DISAGREE A LOT.

A LOT!

DO YOUR PARENTS TELL YOU TO DO THINGS YOU DON'T WANT TO DO?

CERTAINLY! LET ME TELL YOU ABOUT IT...

And then...

17

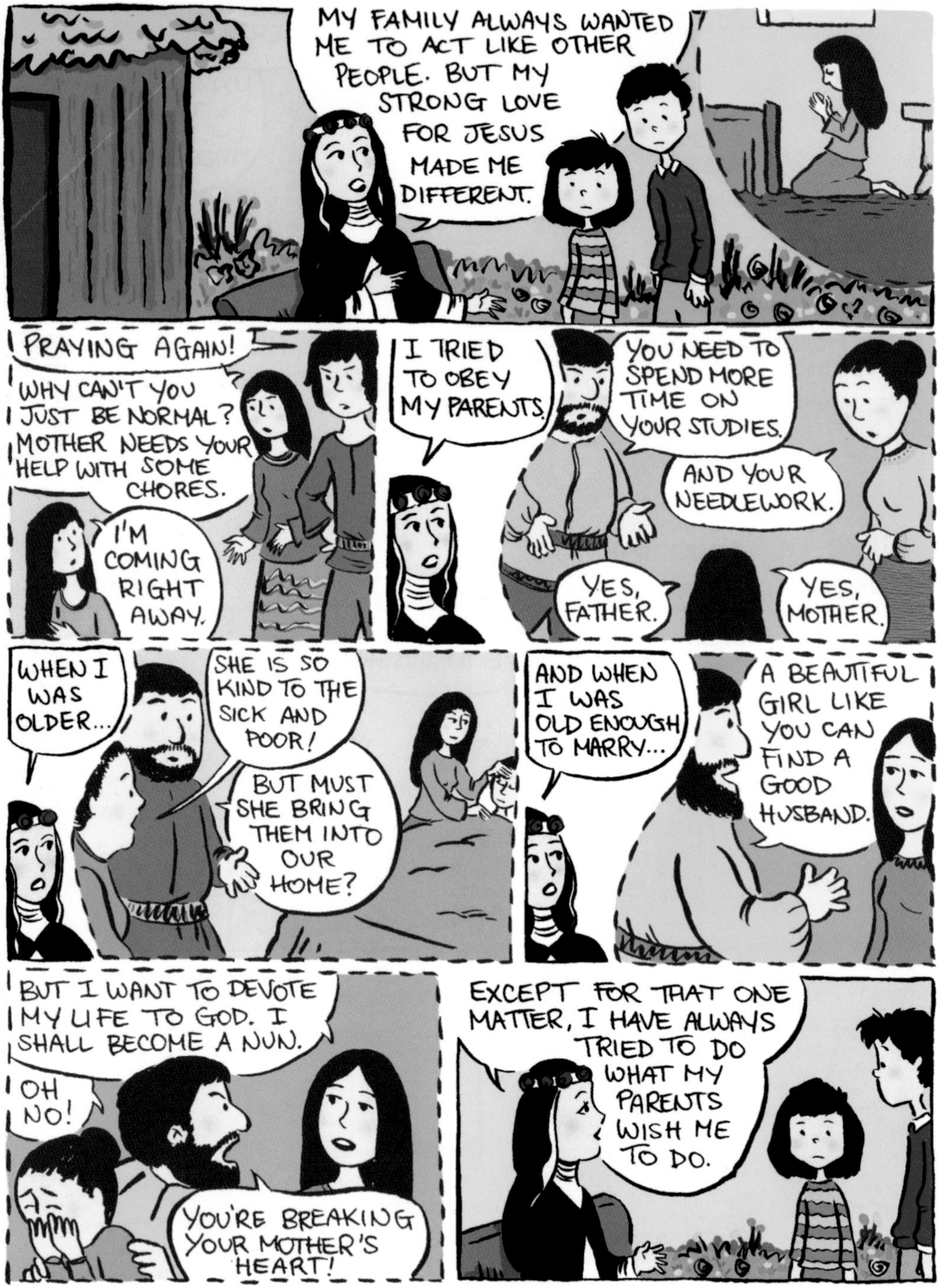
MY FAMILY ALWAYS WANTED ME TO ACT LIKE OTHER PEOPLE. BUT MY STRONG LOVE FOR JESUS MADE ME DIFFERENT.
PRAYING AGAIN!
WHY CAN'T YOU JUST BE NORMAL? MOTHER NEEDS YOUR HELP WITH SOME CHORES.
I'M COMING RIGHT AWAY.
I TRIED TO OBEY MY PARENTS.
YOU NEED TO SPEND MORE TIME ON YOUR STUDIES.
AND YOUR NEEDLEWORK.
YES, FATHER.
YES, MOTHER.
WHEN I WAS OLDER...
SHE IS SO KIND TO THE SICK AND POOR!
BUT MUST SHE BRING THEM INTO OUR HOME?
AND WHEN I WAS OLD ENOUGH TO MARRY...
A BEAUTIFUL GIRL LIKE YOU CAN FIND A GOOD HUSBAND.
BUT I WANT TO DEVOTE MY LIFE TO GOD. I SHALL BECOME A NUN.
OH NO!
YOU'RE BREAKING YOUR MOTHER'S HEART!
EXCEPT FOR THAT ONE MATTER, I HAVE ALWAYS TRIED TO DO WHAT MY PARENTS WISH ME TO DO.

EVEN WHEN YOU DON'T WANT TO?

YES, EVEN THEN.

GOD WANTS US ALL TO HONOR OUR PARENTS. WE DON'T HAVE TO AGREE WITH THEM, BUT WE MUST RESPECT THEM.

I KNOW YOU'RE RIGHT, BUT SOMETIMES...

I HEAR THE FLUTE!

THAT WAS ST. ROSE OF LIMA!

I KNOW! I WISH WE COULD HAVE TALKED TO HER SOME MORE.

SHE WAS THE FIRST SAINT OF THE AMERICAS.

I'D LIKE TO FIND OUT MORE ABOUT HER LIFE.

BUT I'VE ALREADY LEARNED SOMETHING IMPORTANT.

WHAT'S THAT?

TO RESPECT MOM AND DAD. I'M GOING TO CHANGE MY ATTITUDE. RIGHT NOW!

HEY, HOW ABOUT RESPECTING BIG BROTHERS? CECILIA? CECILIA?

But wait... there's more!

"By serving the poor and sick, we serve Jesus."

In 1586, Isabel de Flores y del Oliva was born in Lima, Peru. Her family called her Rose because of her pink cheeks. As Rose grew up, she became even lovelier. She wasn't impressed with herself, though. Her only wish was to be lovely in the eyes of Jesus.

Rose, who became known as "the mother of the poor," was a close friend of another Dominican from Peru who was later named a saint, Martin de Porres. Brother Martin, often called "the apostle of charity," tirelessly provided aid and spiritual counsel to the sick and poor, including enslaved people. Many miracles have been attributed to these two beloved saints.

Because Rose wanted more than anything else to be spiritually beautiful, she spent much of her time in prayer. At a young age, she decided she wanted to dedicate her life to God. She didn't know, however, whether the Lord wanted her to serve him as a religious sister. One day, when she was in the garden of her parent's house, a black and white butterfly landed on her sleeve. Rose believed this was a sign from God to join the Dominican Third Order, whose members wore black and white habits. Because the Third Order is made up of laypersons, she continued to live at home with her family.

With her brother's help, Rose built a small hut in her parents' garden. There she lived simply, sewing lace and embroidering. She also raised vegetables and fruit for the market. With the money she earned, Rose helped the poor people of her town as well as her own family. She often visited the sick and the dying, feeding them, bathing them, and praying with them. Sometimes the people were cured, many believed through miracles.

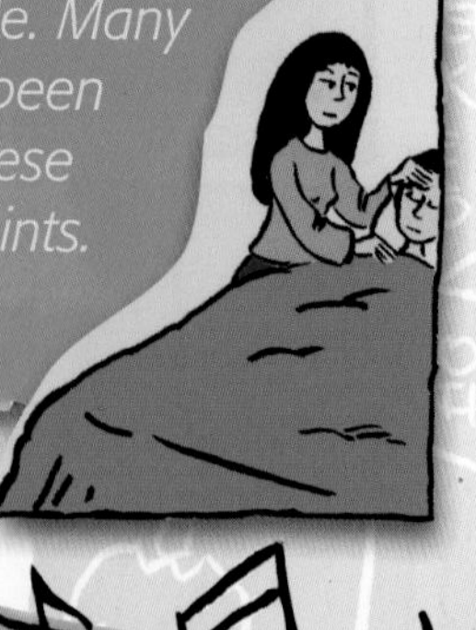

Because of her work among the poor, Saint Rose is known as the founder of social work in Peru.

Pray for the poor of South America, especially for children and for the homeless.

PRAYER

Saint Rose, you became truly beautiful through serving the poor. Help love and kindness to grow in my heart, too.

As Rose prayed and meditated, God often spoke to her in her heart. In time, word of Rose's holiness spread far and wide. Many people visited her town to see her and ask for her blessing. After a long illness, she died at the age of thirty-one, happy to be joining her beloved Jesus at last.

PATRON OF THE AMERICAS
Feast Day
AUGUST 23

Saint Rose of Lima

In 1671, Pope Clement X canonized Rose of Lima as the first saint of the New World.

Saint Sharbel

I'M SO GLAD IT'S SPRING BREAK!

NO SCHOOL!

NO BASKETBALL PRACTICE!

NO FLUTE LESSONS!

NO SCHEDULE AT ALL!!

AND WE FINALLY HAVE TIME TO TRY THE FLUTE AGAIN.

LOOK, PAUL! THE MUSIC CHANGED AGAIN!

LET'S SEE WHERE THIS SONG TAKES US.

IT SURE IS QUIET AROUND HERE.

MAYBE SOMEONE IS INSIDE.

IT MUST BE BORING TO LIVE HERE.

YEAH. THERE ISN'T MUCH TO DO, IS THERE?

WHAT'S IN THERE?

WE SHOULDN'T DISTURB HIM.

LET'S PRAY, TOO.

AH, GUESTS! COME OUTSIDE, CHILDREN!

NOW WHO HAS COME TO VISIT FATHER SHARBEL?

I'M PAUL, FATHER.

AND I'M CECILIA. DO YOU LIVE HERE, FATHER?

YES, I DO. MUCH OF THE TIME I'M ALONE, BUT SOMETIMES OTHER MONKS LIKE TO STAY HERE, TOO.

BUT WHY? THERE'S NOTHING AROUND HERE.

YES. ISN'T IT WONDERFUL?

AND NOTHING TO DO, EITHER.

UH... SURE, FATHER... I GUESS... I... UH...

LET ME EXPLAIN IT TO YOU, CHILDREN.

IT WASN'T EASY GROWING UP IN THE MOUNTAINS OF LEBANON.

WE ALL WORKED HARD TO KEEP OUR FAMILY GOING. I WAS BUSY WITH CHORES ALL THE TIME!

BUT I LOVED TO MAKE TIME FOR PRAYER WHENEVER I COULD.

WHEN I GREW UP, I DECIDED TO BECOME A MONK AND DEVOTE MY LIFE TO GOD.

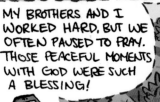

MY BROTHERS AND I WORKED HARD, BUT WE OFTEN PAUSED TO PRAY. THOSE PEACEFUL MOMENTS WITH GOD WERE SUCH A BLESSING!

DO YOU HAVE QUIET TIMES LIKE THAT, CHILDREN?

WE-ELL...WE'RE KIND OF BUSY, FATHER.

THERE'S ALWAYS SOMETHING FOR US TO DO.

I KNOW WHAT YOU MEAN! WHEN WE'RE BUSY, WE FORGET TO MAKE TIME FOR GOD IN OUR LIVES.

I LOVED THE MONASTERY! BUT I FELT BLESSED WHEN I WAS ALLOWED TO GO LIVE A SIMPLE LIFE, ALONE WITH GOD.

I CAN CONCENTRATE ON MY PRAYERS HERE. AND I CAN FEEL GOD'S PEACE INSIDE ME.

IT'S NICE TO SIT QUIETLY FOR A WHILE.

I FEEL LIKE PRAYING NOW.

THEN LET US PRAY.

WOW! ST. SHARBEL REALLY MADE ME THINK.

ME TOO! WE'RE BUSY, BUT WE REALLY NEED TO MAKE TIME FOR GOD.

HOW ABOUT RIGHT NOW? WE COULD FINISH THE PRAYERS WE STARTED WITH ST. SHARBEL.

GOOD IDEA!

NOW LET'S GO HAVE SOME FUN!

YEAH... BEFORE SPRING BREAK IS OVER!

But wait... there's more!

Pray for the people of Lebanon, whose country has been damaged by war.

Saint Sharbel was canonized in 1977 by Pope John VI. Many churches around the world have been named for him.

Yousef Makhlouf was born in a small village in the mountains of Lebanon in 1828. His family was poor, and he was the youngest of five children. When he was only three years old, his father, a mule driver, died. The children were raised in the Maronite Catholic faith by their mother and an uncle.

Yousef took care of his family's sheep and goats. Being outdoors in the pastures helped him to pray and to think of God. Two of Yousef's uncles were monks, and he enjoyed visiting them. When he was twenty-three, he entered a monastery and became a monk himself. He took the religious name Sharbel, sometimes spelled Charbel. Brother Sharbel studied hard and became a priest.

After living in the monastery for sixteen years, Father Sharbel was

Saint Sharbel

Feast Day
DECEMBER 24

salvation of our souls."

Saint Sharbel, help me to remember that I can talk to God any time and any place. Help me to make time for prayer in my life.

granted permission to live as a hermit. He moved to a small hut on a nearby hill where he could be alone and spend most of his time in prayer. He was especially devoted to the Blessed Sacrament and to Mary, the Mother of God. Even though he wanted to spend time by himself, many people came to visit him! They asked for spiritual advice. Many also wanted him to teach them how to pray. Father Sharbel was always kind and welcoming.

Father Sharbel lived as a hermit for twenty-three years. Finally, in 1898, he became ill while celebrating Mass. He died on Christmas Eve, eight days later.

Saint Sharbel was a Maronite Catholic. The Maronite Catholic Church is one of the Eastern Catholic Churches. The Eastern Churches and the Latin Church are united under the bishop of Rome, the Pope. The Eastern Catholic Churches, however, have their own **patriarchs** (head bishops) and different ways of celebrating the liturgy.

After Father Sharbel's death, people began to see dazzling lights around his grave. Many miracles have been attributed to him.

Saint Monica

HEY, BETH IS LOOKING FOR YOU.

I KNOW! THAT'S WHY I CAME UP HERE WHERE SHE'S NOT ALLOWED!

IS BETH BOTHERING YOU?

SHE SURE IS! SHE COPIES EVERYTHING I DO!

WELL, YOU'RE HER BIG BROTHER. SHE LOOKS UP TO YOU.

BUT SHE'S DRIVING ME NUTS! IF I DON'T EAT MY CARROTS, THEN SHE WON'T EAT HER CARROTS!

IF I DON'T MAKE MY BED, SHE DOESN'T MAKE HERS. SHE TALKS LIKE ME, TOO, AND—

OKAY, OKAY!

LET'S SEE IF THE...YES! THE MUSIC CHANGED AGAIN!

TRY IT AND SEE WHAT HAPPENS.

COULD THIS BE AFRICA?

MAYBE THAT LADY CAN HELP US.

EXCUSE ME, MA'AM. DID YOU JUST ARRIVE HERE?

NO, AFRICA IS MY HOME. I'M SAILING TO ROME TO SEE MY SON.

WOW! THAT'S A LONG TRIP!

IT'S WORTH IT TO SEE MY SON. I'VE WORRIED ABOUT AUGUSTINE ALL HIS LIFE.

AUGUSTINE! THAT'S OUR BABY BROTHER'S NAME!

HOW NICE!

WHY ARE YOU WORRIED ABOUT YOUR SON?

AUGUSTINE IS NOT A CHRISTIAN. I DO SO WISH HE WOULD ACCEPT THE LORD AND LIVE A RIGHTEOUS LIFE.

IS YOUR HUSBAND A CHRISTIAN?

OH! WE'RE SORRY TO HEAR THAT.

MY HUSBAND PASSED AWAY SOME YEARS AGO.

THANK YOU, DEAR. TO ANSWER YOUR QUESTION, MY HUSBAND WASN'T CHRISTIAN WHEN I MARRIED HIM. AND NEITHER WAS MY MOTHER-IN-LAW.

BUT I HELPED THEM CHANGE. AND I DIDN'T EVEN KNOW I WAS DOING IT!

REALLY?

HOW DID YOU DO THAT?

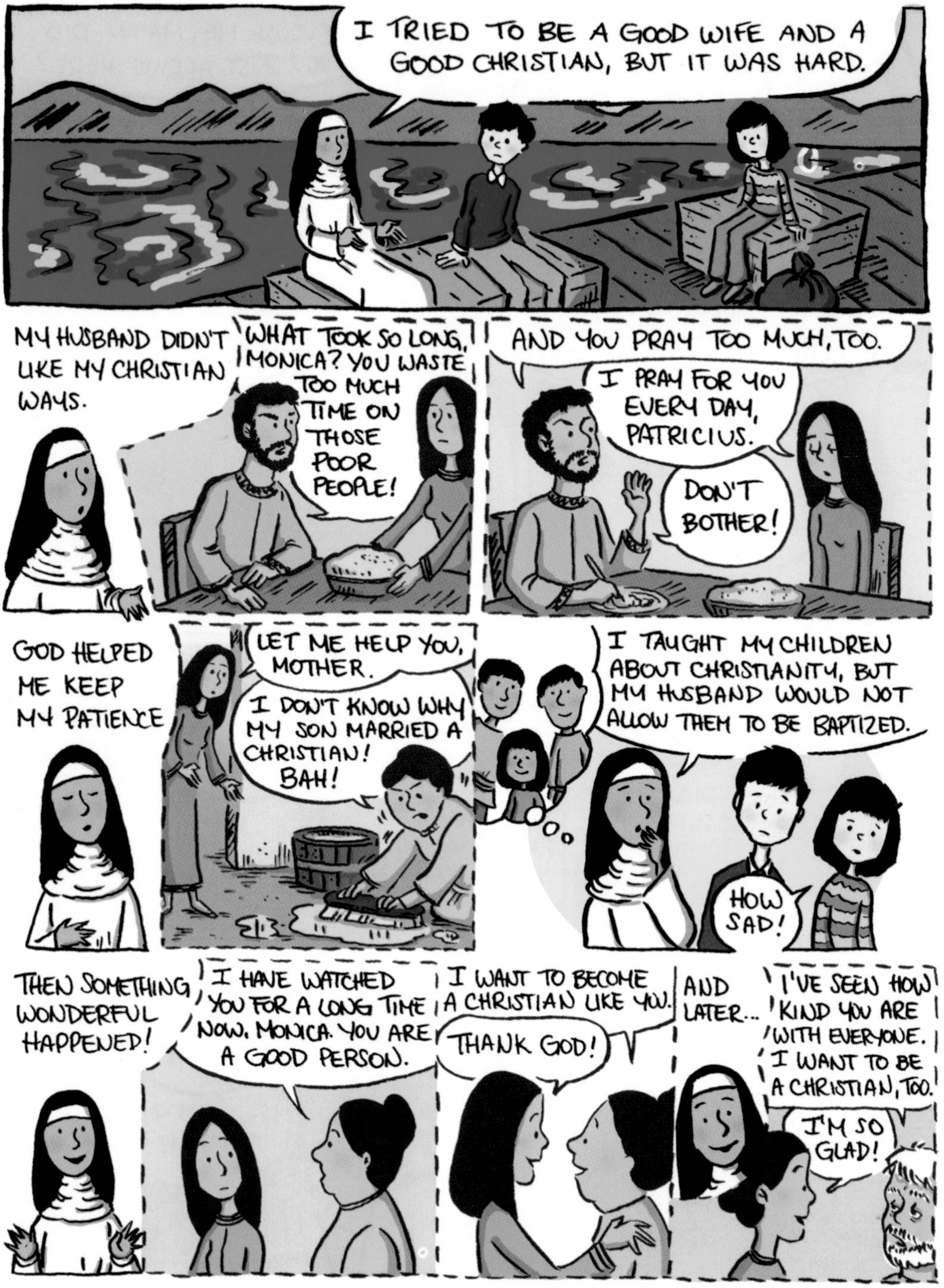

I TRIED TO BE A GOOD WIFE AND A GOOD CHRISTIAN, BUT IT WAS HARD.
MY HUSBAND DIDN'T LIKE MY CHRISTIAN WAYS.
WHAT TOOK SO LONG, MONICA? YOU WASTE TOO MUCH TIME ON THOSE POOR PEOPLE!
AND YOU PRAY TOO MUCH, TOO.
I PRAY FOR YOU EVERY DAY, PATRICIUS.
DON'T BOTHER!
GOD HELPED ME KEEP MY PATIENCE
LET ME HELP YOU, MOTHER.
I DON'T KNOW WHY MY SON MARRIED A CHRISTIAN! BAH!
I TAUGHT MY CHILDREN ABOUT CHRISTIANITY, BUT MY HUSBAND WOULD NOT ALLOW THEM TO BE BAPTIZED.
HOW SAD!
THEN SOMETHING WONDERFUL HAPPENED!
I HAVE WATCHED YOU FOR A LONG TIME NOW, MONICA. YOU ARE A GOOD PERSON.
I WANT TO BECOME A CHRISTIAN LIKE YOU.
THANK GOD!
AND LATER...
I'VE SEEN HOW KIND YOU ARE WITH EVERYONE. I WANT TO BE A CHRISTIAN, TOO.
I'M SO GLAD!

I DIDN'T REALIZE THEY WERE WATCHING ME SO CLOSELY!

HMMM...

AUGUSTINE'S BROTHER AND SISTER ALSO BECAME CHRISTIANS.

WOW! YOU REALLY HAD AN EFFECT ON PEOPLE.

I DIDN'T KNOW I WAS A ROLE MODEL!

I BET AUGUSTINE WILL BECOME A CHRISTIAN, TOO...

UH-OH! THE MUSIC!

YOU WERE RIGHT ABOUT ST. MONICA'S SON. HE DID BECOME A CHRISTIAN. HE WAS ST. AUGUSTINE!

WOW!

I SHOULD BE MORE CAREFUL HOW I ACT AROUND BETH. I COULD BE AN IMPORTANT ROLE MODEL FOR HER.

AND FOR YOU, TOO.

WHATEVER!

But wait... there's more!

"Remember me at the altar of the Lord."

PATRON OF MOTHERS, CONVERTS
Feast Day
AUGUST 27

Monica prayed for years that Augustine, her oldest son, would change his way of living. Her prayers were answered when he became not just a good Christian, but also a priest, a fine preacher, a bishop, a great writer, and, eventually, a famous saint himself! We celebrate his feast day on August 28, the day after Monica's.

Monica was born around 332 in North Africa to Christian parents. At the age of twenty-two, she married Patricius, a much older man. Soon they had two young sons and a daughter—Augustine, Navigius, and Perpetua. Although her husband wasn't Christian, Monica taught her children to pray and to love Jesus.

When Augustine was a teenager, he was sent to another city to go to school. There he fell into bad company and began to lie, cheat, steal—and worse. His father had died soon after being baptized a Christian. Without her husband's help, Monica grew more and more worried about her oldest son.

Augustine, a brilliant scholar, eventually began studying in Carthage, a large city. To Monica's dismay, he joined a religious group that didn't believe in the true God. Although she begged him to reconsider, Augustine stubbornly refused to return to Christianity. Monica didn't give up, though. She continued to pray for him, asking God to open her son's eyes to the truth. Finally, Augustine left Carthage, taking a ship to Rome, where he planned to become a teacher of public speaking.

Mothers everywhere pray to Saint Monica for the welfare of their children.

Soon Augustine moved to Milan, where he heard the sermons of a Christian bishop named Ambrose. Finally he decided that Ambrose—and Monica—were right. Christianity really was the only true faith! He was baptized on Easter Sunday in 387.

Monica, who had joined him in Milan, was very happy. Soon after, though, she became seriously ill. Nine days later she died, secure at last in knowing that she would someday see her beloved son in heaven.

Most of what we know about Saint Monica comes from the writings of Saint Augustine. As he grew older, he came to appreciate his mother's devotion more and more.

Saint Monica

Pray that everyone, even people who say they don't believe in religion, will become aware of God's love.

PRAYER

Saint Monica, you kept your faith and prayed for years because you loved your son so much. Help me to be patient and loving, too.

33

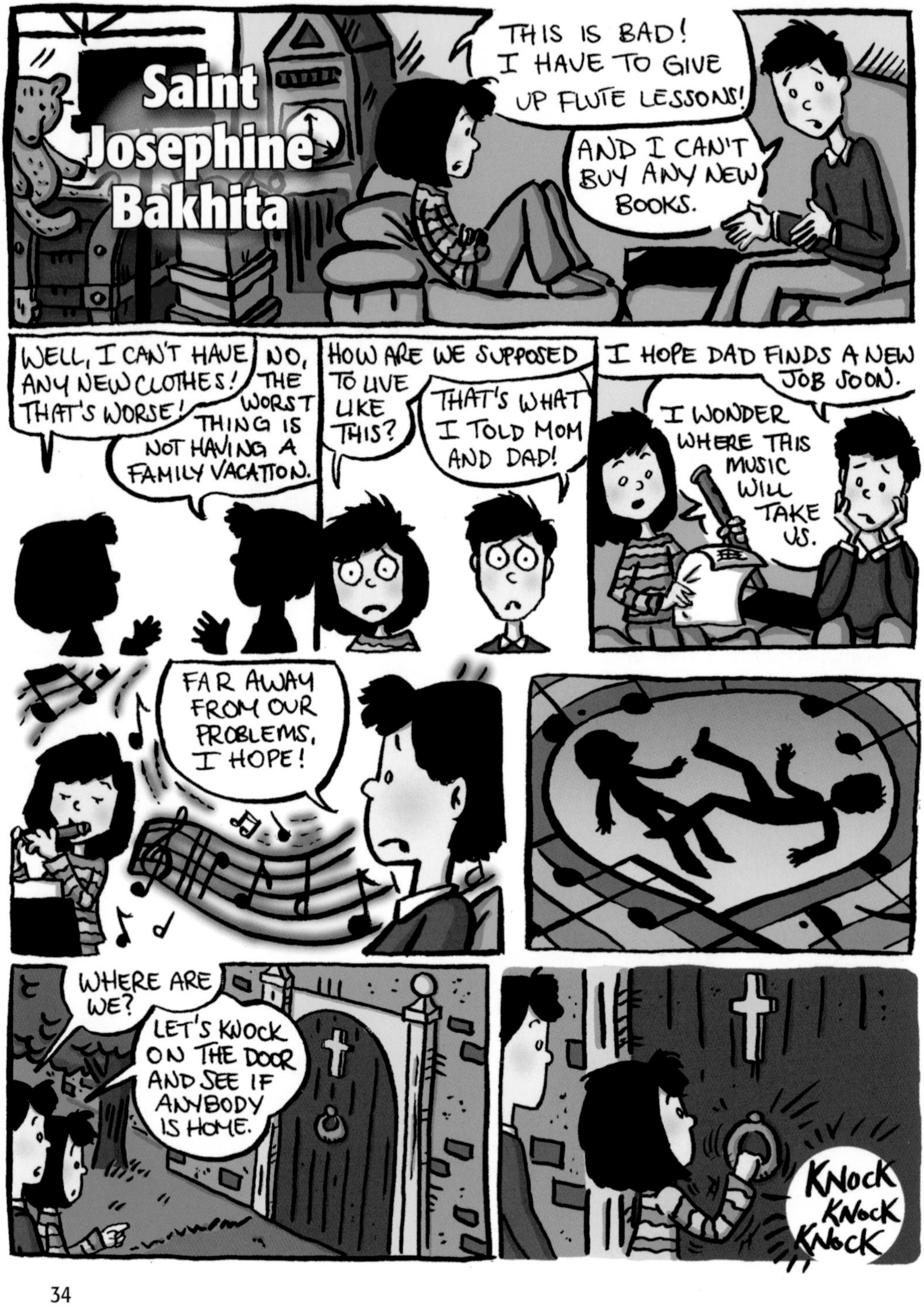
Saint Josephine Bakhita
THIS IS BAD! I HAVE TO GIVE UP FLUTE LESSONS!
AND I CAN'T BUY ANY NEW BOOKS.
WELL, I CAN'T HAVE ANY NEW CLOTHES! THAT'S WORSE!
NO, THE WORST THING IS NOT HAVING A FAMILY VACATION.
HOW ARE WE SUPPOSED TO LIVE LIKE THIS?
THAT'S WHAT I TOLD MOM AND DAD!
I HOPE DAD FINDS A NEW JOB SOON.
I WONDER WHERE THIS MUSIC WILL TAKE US.
FAR AWAY FROM OUR PROBLEMS, I HOPE!
WHERE ARE WE?
LET'S KNOCK ON THE DOOR AND SEE IF ANYBODY IS HOME.
KNOCK KNOCK KNOCK

WELCOME, CHILDREN! CAN I HELP YOU? DO YOU NEED FOOD?

NO SISTER,... WE... WE...

WE JUST WANTED TO TALK!

THEN COME IN!

I CAN SEE YOU ARE WORRIED ABOUT SOMETHING. SIT DOWN AND TELL SISTER JOSEPHINE WHAT IS BOTHERING YOU.

WE HAVE A TERRIBLE PROBLEM, SISTER!

OUR FATHER LOST HIS JOB.

OH! NO WONDER YOU ARE WORRIED.

I DON'T UNDERSTAND WHY GOD LET THIS HAPPEN TO US!

ME NEITHER! I THOUGHT GOD LOVED US.

HE DOES LOVE YOU!

AND HE HAS A PLAN FOR YOU—AND FOR EVERYONE ELSE, TOO.

I SURE DON'T UNDERSTAND HIS PLAN.

THAT'S ALL RIGHT. YOU CAN TRUST THAT HE KNOWS WHAT IS RIGHT FOR YOU.

BUT WE DON'T HAVE ENOUGH MONEY!

HOW CAN THAT BE RIGHT FOR US?

MAYBE IT WILL HELP IF I TELL YOU ABOUT GOD'S PLAN FOR ME.

WHEN I WAS A LITTLE GIRL IN SUDAN, AFRICA, I KNEW NOTHING ABOUT GOD. I DIDN'T EVEN KNOW HE EXISTED!

WOW!

ONE DAY, SOME MEN KIDNAPPED ME AND SOLD ME AS A SLAVE. I NEVER SAW MY FAMILY AGAIN.

LET ME GO!

LIFE AS A SLAVE WAS VERY HARD.

DO A GOOD JOB OR YOU'LL GET A BEATING.

YES, MA'AM.

I WAS SOLD SEVERAL TIMES OVER THE YEARS, BUT MY LIFE DID NOT GET BETTER.

CLUMSY GIRL! I'LL PUNISH YOU!

ONE OF MY OWNERS BEAT ME SO BADLY I HAD TO STAY IN BED FOR A MONTH.

FINALLY I WENT TO A KIND FAMILY IN ITALY.

WE'RE SO HAPPY TO HAVE YOU TAKING CARE OF BABY MIMMINA.

I LOVE HER!

WHEN MIMMINA WAS OLDER, I WENT WITH HER TO A CONVENT SCHOOL IN ITALY. THAT'S WHERE I FINALLY LEARNED ABOUT GOD!

I WAS SO HAPPY— UNTIL MIMMINA'S PARENTS CAME TO TAKE US BACK TO SUDAN.

I WANT TO STAY HERE AND BE BAPTIZED.

BUT YOU ARE OUR PROPERTY.

LET'S SEE WHAT THE LAW SAYS ABOUT THAT.

PEOPLE AREN'T PROPERTY!

LUCKY FOR ME, THE LAW WAS IN MY FAVOR! TO MY GREAT JOY, I BECAME A CATHOLIC, AND LATER, A SISTER.

SO YOU SEE... GOD MADE SOMETHING VERY GOOD COME OUT OF SOMETHING BAD! HE HAD A PLAN FOR ME ALL ALONG.

THAT'S AMAZING!

WOW!

SAINT JOSEPHINE BAKHITA HAD A ROUGH LIFE!

YES, BUT GOD MADE HIS PLAN WORK OUT ANYWAY!

HE'LL DO THAT FOR US, TOO.

RIGHT! GOD LOVES US! WE CAN TRUST THAT HE HAS A PLAN.

HEY! I HAVE A PLAN, TOO! I'M GOING TO SHOW MOM AND DAD A BETTER ATTITUDE ABOUT OUR TROUBLES.

AND I'M STARTING RIGHT NOW!

ME, TOO!

STORMS

But wait...there's more!

37

Saint Josephine Bakhita

Saint Bakhita was so young when she was kidnapped that she forgot her birth name. She used the name slave traders gave her—Bakhita—which means "lucky one."

PATRON OF WORKERS, SUDAN
Feast Day
FEBRUARY 8

This saint was born around 1869 in a small village in the Darfur region of Sudan, the largest country in Africa. When Bakhita was seven years old, she was lured away from her village by Arab slave traders. Kidnapped, torn from her family and friends, the frightened young girl would spend the next nine years of her life as a slave.

Bakhita was treated relatively kindly by a few owners, but others were much crueler. She was routinely beaten, starved, and treated harshly. When Bakhita was a teenager, her owner, a Turkish general, decided to sell her once again. The girl was shocked. What if her new situation was even worse?

Fortunately, Bakhita entered the household of Signor Lignani, an Italian government official. When he returned to Italy, he brought sixteen-year-old Bakhita with him. In Italy, Bakhita cared for the young daughter of the Michieli family. She eventually attended a boarding school run by the Canossian Sisters. There she learned about Jesus. Later, the Michielis decided to return to Africa.

great peace."

Pray for the people of the Sudan, whose country has been torn by war, famine, and disease.

PRAYER

Saint Bakhita, even though your life was hard, you always trusted in God and never gave up. Please share your forgiving heart with me.

Bakhita, knowing that slavery was illegal in Italy, refused to go with them. The Canossian Sisters agreed that she could stay at school and receive Baptism. At last—freedom!

In 1893, Bakhita entered the congregation of the Canossian Sisters. With great love, she served the Lord and her community as Sister Josephine Bakhita for over fifty years. Her autobiography, *A Wonderful Story*, was published in 1931. It allowed others to learn about her amazing life. In fact, because of her story, quite a few young women decided to join the Canossian congregation. In 1947, this gentle sister peacefully died. We honor Saint Bakhita today for her loving heart and her astonishing ability to forgive all those who had wronged her.

Although Christianity was first brought to Africa by missionaries in the mid-1800s, Bakhita's family had never heard of Jesus. Disease and poverty made it difficult to preach the Gospel in this part of the continent. The peaceful, hardworking people of Bakhita's tribe followed traditional African beliefs.

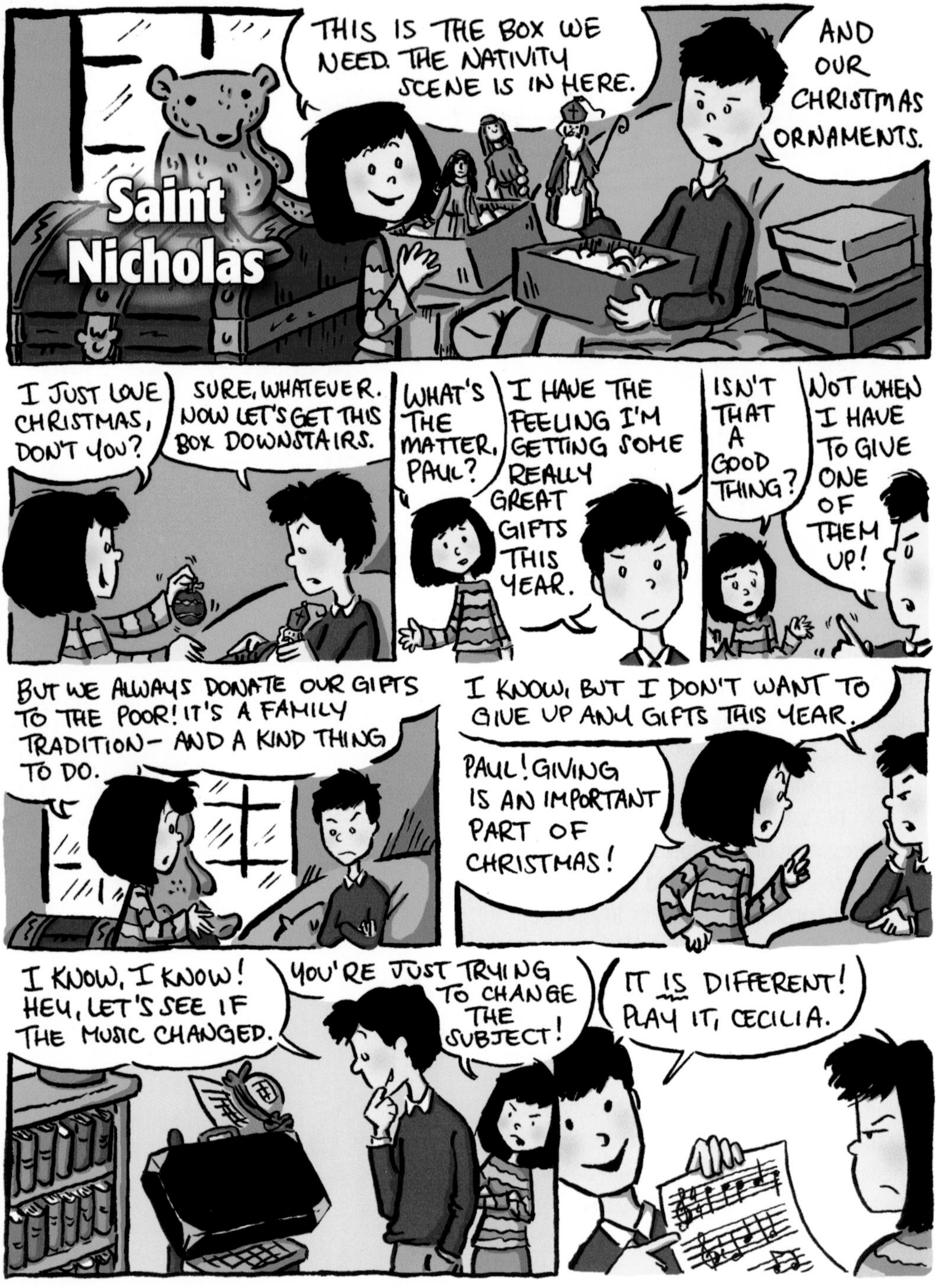
Saint Nicholas
THIS IS THE BOX WE NEED. THE NATIVITY SCENE IS IN HERE.
AND OUR CHRISTMAS ORNAMENTS.
I JUST LOVE CHRISTMAS, DON'T YOU?
SURE, WHATEVER. NOW LET'S GET THIS BOX DOWNSTAIRS.
WHAT'S THE MATTER, PAUL?
I HAVE THE FEELING I'M GETTING SOME REALLY GREAT GIFTS THIS YEAR.
ISN'T THAT A GOOD THING?
NOT WHEN I HAVE TO GIVE ONE OF THEM UP!
BUT WE ALWAYS DONATE OUR GIFTS TO THE POOR! IT'S A FAMILY TRADITION— AND A KIND THING TO DO.
I KNOW, BUT I DON'T WANT TO GIVE UP ANY GIFTS THIS YEAR.
PAUL! GIVING IS AN IMPORTANT PART OF CHRISTMAS!
I KNOW, I KNOW! HEY, LET'S SEE IF THE MUSIC CHANGED.
YOU'RE JUST TRYING TO CHANGE THE SUBJECT!
IT IS DIFFERENT! PLAY IT, CECILIA.

OH, ALL RIGHT.

WHERE ARE WE?

LOOK, PAUL! IS THAT A ROBBER?

HE'S GOING TO BREAK THE GLASS AND GET INTO THE HOUSE!

I DIDN'T HEAR ANYTHING.

LONG AGO, WINDOWS DIDN'T HAVE GLASS.

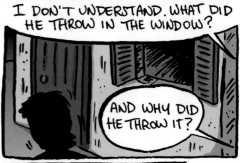

I DON'T UNDERSTAND. WHAT DID HE THROW IN THE WINDOW?

AND WHY DID HE THROW IT?

STOP! STOP!

FINALLY I CAUGHT YOU!

And then...

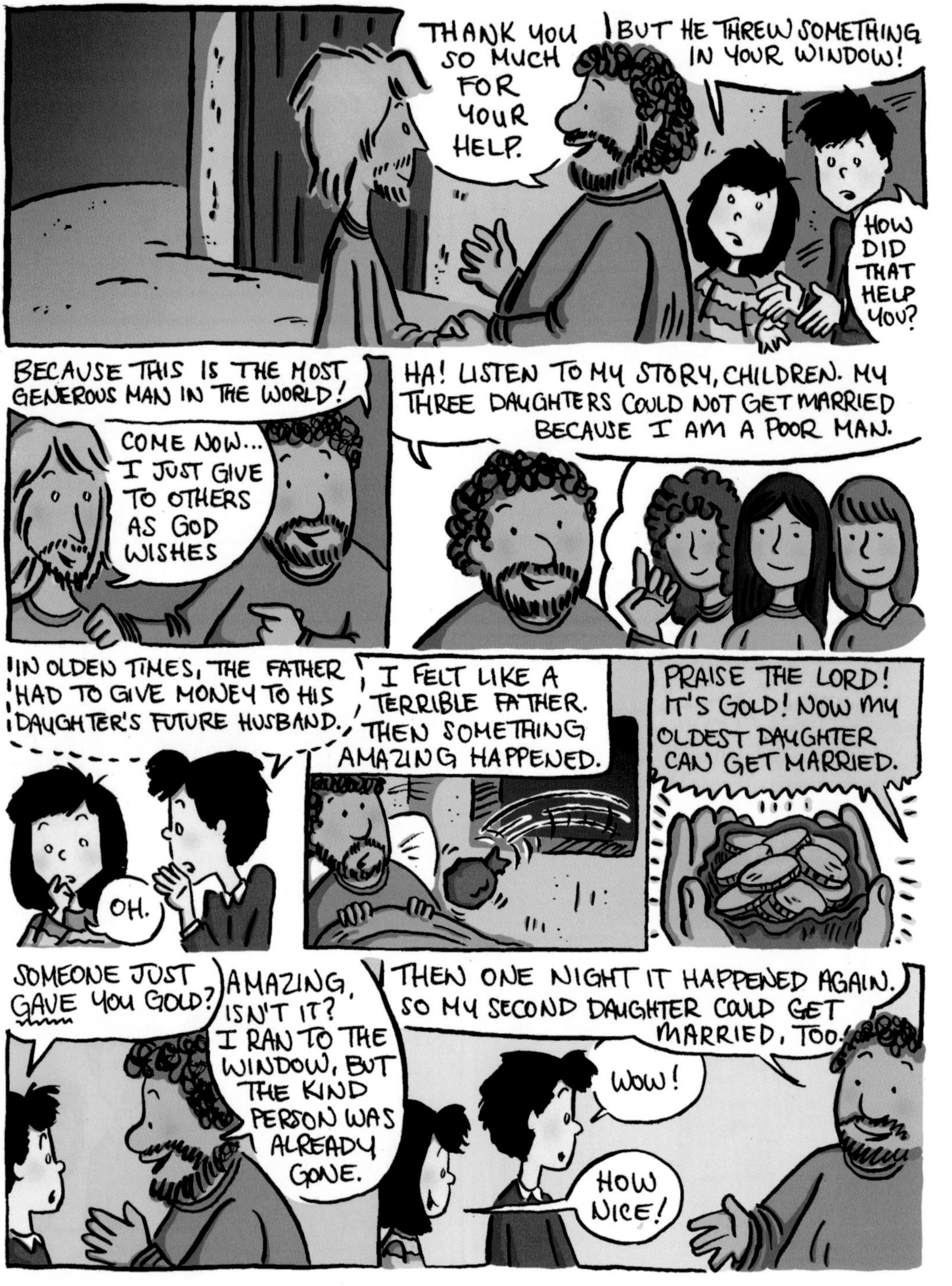
THANK YOU SO MUCH FOR YOUR HELP.
BUT HE THREW SOMETHING IN YOUR WINDOW!
HOW DID THAT HELP YOU?
BECAUSE THIS IS THE MOST GENEROUS MAN IN THE WORLD!
COME NOW... I JUST GIVE TO OTHERS AS GOD WISHES
HA! LISTEN TO MY STORY, CHILDREN. MY THREE DAUGHTERS COULD NOT GET MARRIED BECAUSE I AM A POOR MAN.
IN OLDEN TIMES, THE FATHER HAD TO GIVE MONEY TO HIS DAUGHTER'S FUTURE HUSBAND.
OH.
I FELT LIKE A TERRIBLE FATHER. THEN SOMETHING AMAZING HAPPENED.
PRAISE THE LORD! IT'S GOLD! NOW MY OLDEST DAUGHTER CAN GET MARRIED.
SOMEONE JUST GAVE YOU GOLD?
AMAZING, ISN'T IT? I RAN TO THE WINDOW, BUT THE KIND PERSON WAS ALREADY GONE.
THEN ONE NIGHT IT HAPPENED AGAIN. SO MY SECOND DAUGHTER COULD GET MARRIED, TOO.
WOW!
HOW NICE!

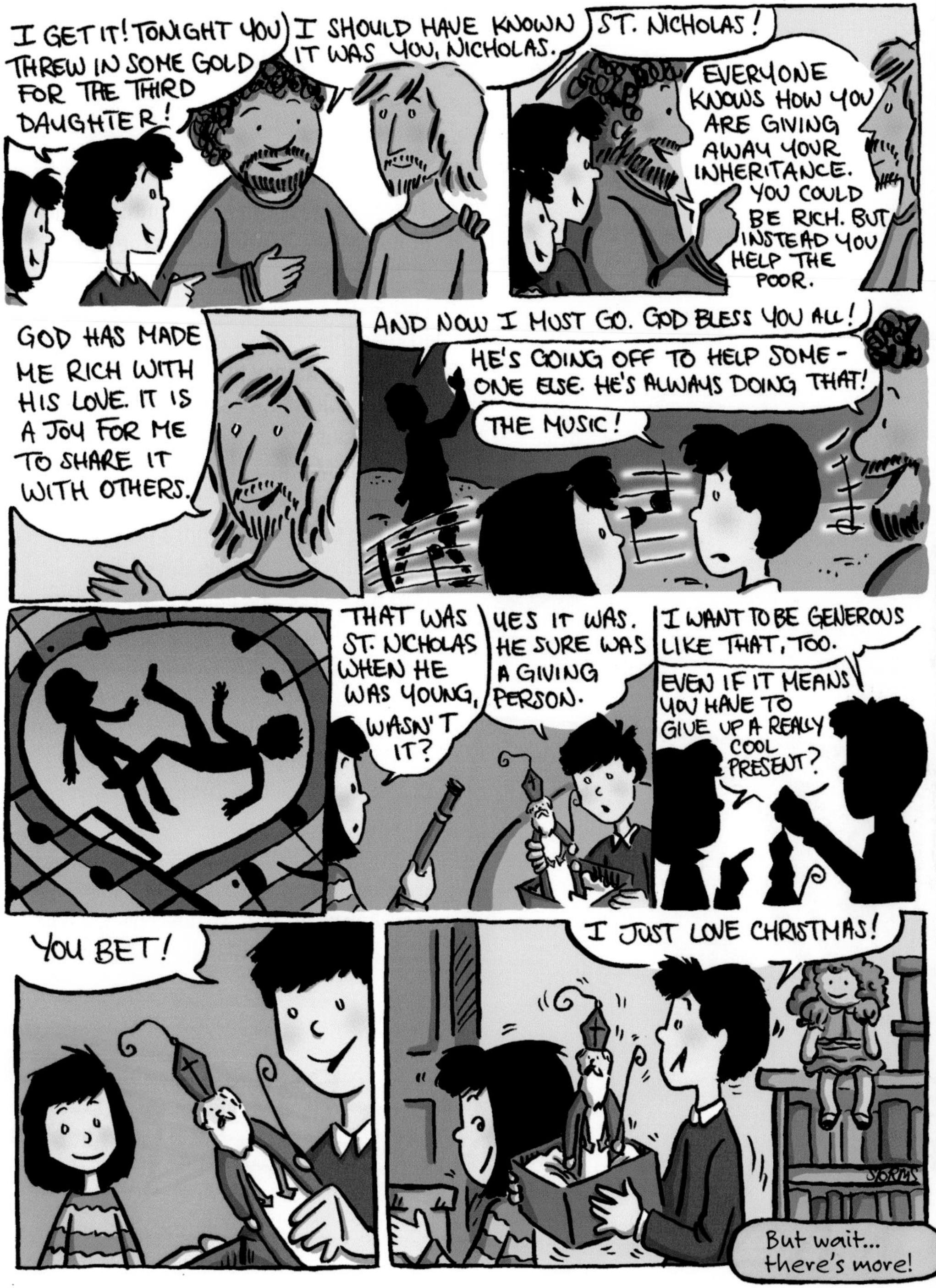

I GET IT! TONIGHT YOU THREW IN SOME GOLD FOR THE THIRD DAUGHTER!
I SHOULD HAVE KNOWN IT WAS YOU, NICHOLAS.
ST. NICHOLAS!
EVERYONE KNOWS HOW YOU ARE GIVING AWAY YOUR INHERITANCE. YOU COULD BE RICH. BUT INSTEAD YOU HELP THE POOR.
GOD HAS MADE ME RICH WITH HIS LOVE. IT IS A JOY FOR ME TO SHARE IT WITH OTHERS.
AND NOW I MUST GO. GOD BLESS YOU ALL!
HE'S GOING OFF TO HELP SOMEONE ELSE. HE'S ALWAYS DOING THAT!
THE MUSIC!
THAT WAS ST. NICHOLAS WHEN HE WAS YOUNG, WASN'T IT?
YES IT WAS. HE SURE WAS A GIVING PERSON.
I WANT TO BE GENEROUS LIKE THAT, TOO.
EVEN IF IT MEANS YOU HAVE TO GIVE UP A REALLY COOL PRESENT?
YOU BET!
I JUST LOVE CHRISTMAS!
STORMS
But wait... there's more!

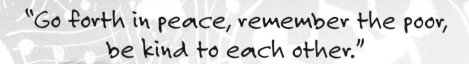

"Go forth in peace, remember the poor, be kind to each other."

Pray that all the men and women at sea may be brought safely home to their loved ones.

Saint Nicholas

Nicholas was born in the fourth century in Asia Minor, which today is the country of Turkey. His family was wealthy. When Nicholas's parents died, he didn't want to keep their riches to himself. Instead he gave all his money to charity.

Later Nicholas became a bishop. He was famous for his fairness and devotion to justice. Many miracles are attributed to him. Once, when he was on a ship traveling to the Holy Land, a terrible storm blew up. Nicholas stayed calm. "We must pray," he told the sailors. Sure enough, the storm quickly calmed and the ship was saved! This story is the reason so many sailors and dockworkers are devoted to Saint Nicholas.

When Bishop Nicholas died, a great church was built over his tomb in Myra, Turkey.

There are many legends about this well-loved saint. Here is a famous one:

Many years after Nicholas died, a band of pirates from the island of Crete came to

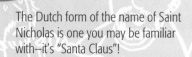

The Dutch form of the name of Saint Nicholas is one you may be familiar with—it's "Santa Claus"!

Saint Nicholas, you had a generous and loving heart. Help me to be a kind person and to do good things for others, as you did.

PATRON OF CHILDREN, PRISONERS, BOATMEN, RUSSIA
Feast Day
DECEMBER 6

Myra. On the feast of Saint Nicholas, they robbed the church of its treasures. As they were leaving, they kidnapped a young boy named Basil. Basil was made a slave to the emir, or king. One of his duties was to bring the emir his wine in a beautiful cup made of gold.

Meanwhile, Basil's parents, of course, were terribly sad! They worried about their lost son. On the next feast of Saint Nicholas, Basil's mother stayed home and prayed for his safety. At the same time, in Crete, Saint Nicholas appeared to Basil. He blessed the boy, whisked him through the air, and set him down at his home in Myra. When Basil magically appeared to his parents, he was still holding the king's golden cup! This legend is one reason Saint Nicholas came to be known as a protector of children.

Saint Nicholas's feast day is in December, early in Advent. In many countries, on the evening before, children leave shoes or stockings for Saint Nicholas to fill during the night. The next morning, they find small gifts as well as fruit, nuts, and special candies. Saint Nicholas's gifts are always meant to be shared with others!

In 1087, Saint Nicholas's body was moved to Bari, Italy—some say by thieves. His relics are still preserved there in the church of San Nicola.

45

Saint Teresa of Avila

HEY, LOOK! THERE'S A BIG SALE! WE CAN PUT OUR MONEY TOGETHER AND GET MOM THIS WATCH FOR HER BIRTHDAY.

IT'S NICE, BUT I... UH... I MEAN...

WHAT'S WRONG?

SORRY, BUT I DON'T HAVE ANY MONEY.

OH. HEY, WAIT A MINUTE! ISN'T THAT A NEW SWEATER?

IT'S THE LATEST THING. ISN'T IT CUTE?

CECILIA! YOU CAN'T KEEP SPENDING MONEY ON CLOTHES!

I HAVE TO DO IT, OR I WON'T BE IN STYLE!

SO?

YOU JUST DON'T GET IT! LET'S TRY THE FLUTE.

WOW! LOOK AT THAT FANTASTIC DRESS!

AREN'T THESE BEAUTIFUL CLOTHES? OOH I LOVE THESE SHOES!

HEY, STAY OUT OF THERE!

I CAN'T BELIEVE HE SAID NO!

I HAVE TO DO WHAT GOD CALLS ME TO DO - EVEN IF FATHER DOESN'T AGREE!

OH, MY! WHAT ARE YOU DOING HERE, CHILDREN?

WE'RE...UH... WE'RE...OH....

VISITORS!

I LOVE VISITORS! IT'S SO MUCH FUN MEETING NEW PEOPLE AND TALKING TO THEM!

BUT I'M AFRAID I DON'T HAVE TIME FOR THAT RIGHT NOW. I HAVE TO GET READY TO GO AWAY.

SO DO YOU NEED HELP PACKING ALL YOUR LOVELY OUTFITS?

NO, I WON'T BE NEEDING THEM.

THESE FANCY CLOTHES ARE PART OF THE REASON I'M LEAVING HOME - FOREVER!

BUT HOW CAN PRETTY CLOTHES MAKE YOU LEAVE HOME?

I DIDN'T MEAN THAT! LET ME EXPLAIN.

MY PARENTS TAUGHT ME THAT LOVING GOD AND BEING A GOOD PERSON ARE THE MOST IMPORTANT THINGS IN LIFE.

BUT AS I GREW OLDER, I VALUED THE WRONG THINGS.

STOP WASTING TIME ON THOSE SILLY NOVELS, TERESA!

BUT THEY'RE SO ROMANTIC!

LOOK AT THIS BEAUTIFUL FABRIC! PLEASE BUY IT FOR ME, FATHER!

OH... ALL RIGHT.

I DON'T HAVE ANYTHING TO WEAR! I'LL ASK FATHER IF I CAN HAVE A NEW DRESS MADE.

I LOVE YOUR DRESS!

IT'S THE LATEST FASHION, YOU KNOW.

YOU'RE THE BEST-DRESSED GIRL IN AVILA!

ALL I CARED ABOUT WAS HAVING FUN AND GOSSIPING AND SHOWING OFF AND LOOKING STYLISH.

BUT THERE'S NOTHING WRONG WITH BEING IN STYLE IS THERE?

NO, BUT I'VE BEEN MAKING IT TOO IMPORTANT.

I'VE BECOME SELF-CENTERED AND VAIN. I KEEP FORGETTING ABOUT WHAT REALLY MATTERS.

BUT I'VE DECIDED TO CHANGE. I FEEL CALLED TO BECOME A NUN AND MAKE MY LIFE MEAN SOMETHING.

FATHER DOESN'T WANT ME TO DO IT, BUT I WILL!

THE MUSIC!

WOW! WHEN ST. TERESA OF AVILA WAS YOUNG, SHE LIKED A LOT OF THE SAME THINGS THAT KIDS DO TODAY.

YES, BUT SHE LEARNED NOT TO CARE ABOUT THAT STUFF TOO MUCH. THERE ARE MORE IMPORTANT THINGS IN LIFE.

MOM IS IMPORTANT TO ME. I'LL RETURN SOMETHING I HAVEN'T WORN YET, AND GET MONEY FOR HER BIRTHDAY GIFT.

GREAT!

BUT LET'S GET HER A DIFFERENT WATCH. THE ONE IN THE NEWSPAPER IS SO OUT OF STYLE!

But wait...there's more!

"All things pass; God never changes."

PATRON OF HEADACHE
SUFFERERS, SPAIN
Feast Day
OCTOBER 15

Pray for sisters, nuns, brothers, and priests who dedicate their lives to helping others.

When Teresa was seven, she and her brother decided that the surest way to get to heaven would be to become martyrs. They tried to run away to Africa, where they hoped to die for Christ. Fortunately they were brought home before they got too far! Teresa's father helped them to understand that we can all get to heaven by loving God.

Teresa was born in Avila, Spain, on March 28, 1515. When she was a teenager, her mother died. Teresa missed her very much, so much that she took to reading romantic adventure novels as a way of escaping her sadness. She and her brother Rodriguez even wrote a novel themselves! They decided it wasn't very good, though, and never showed it to anyone.

As Teresa grew older, she became foolish and vain. The pretty teenager started spending too much of her time thinking about friends, parties, and boys. Her father finally decided to send her to a boarding school run by the Augustinian sisters. There, after a time, Teresa began to consider becoming a nun herself.

At the age of twenty-one, after a serious illness, Teresa entered the

Doctor of the Church is a title given to very few. It honors saints whose writings and teachings have benefited Catholics everywhere.

Teresa of Avila was canonized by Pope Gregory XV in 1622. In 1970, Pope Paul VI declared her to be the first woman Doctor of the Church.

Carmelite Order. She often found it hard to pray and to be as close to God as she wanted to be. Finally, after many years, God gave Teresa the grace of actually hearing Jesus speak to her in her heart. Teresa understood then that the Lord was asking more of her.

Following God's will, Teresa led a reform among the Carmelites by founding new convents for nuns and monasteries for friars. These reformed religious were known as the Discalced (that means "without shoes") Carmelites. They went back to living, working, and praying by an older rule that was much stricter and less worldly than what the other Carmelites followed. They embraced a life of poverty, prayer, and love, just as Jesus did.

By the time Teresa died in 1582, she had, with the help of another famous Carmelite, Saint John of the Cross, begun sixteen convents and two monasteries. When she died, the citizens of Avila told one another, "A great saint has gone to heaven."

Saint Teresa of Avila

PRAYER

Saint Teresa, help me to remember to pray each day with attention and love. Help me to hold Jesus and the Blessed Mother in my heart always.

Saint John Bosco

THESE OLD DISHES ARE SO PRETTY. AND THIS FAKE FRUIT LOOKS ALMOST REAL!

HEY, AREN'T YOU SUPPOSED TO BE MEETING WITH YOUR CLUB RIGHT NOW?

THE MEETING'S OVER! THEY ALL WENT HOME.

SLAM!!

WHAT HAPPENED?

NOBODY WOULD LISTEN TO ME WHEN WE STARTED BUILDING OUR TREE HOUSE!

I KNOW ALL ABOUT WOOD WORKING, BUT THEY WOULDN'T DO ANYTHING I SAID.

IMAGINE THAT!

I STARTED THAT CLUB FOR MY FRIENDS, BUT THEY WOULDN'T COOPERATE. THEN THEY ALL QUIT ON ME!

GEE, I WONDER WHY.

WHAT'S THAT SUPPOSED TO MEAN?

I GET TIRED OF YOU ORDERING ME AROUND. YOU'RE TOO BOSSY!

I BET YOUR FRIENDS FEEL THE SAME WAY.

I AM NOT BOSSY! HERE! PLAY THE FLUTE!

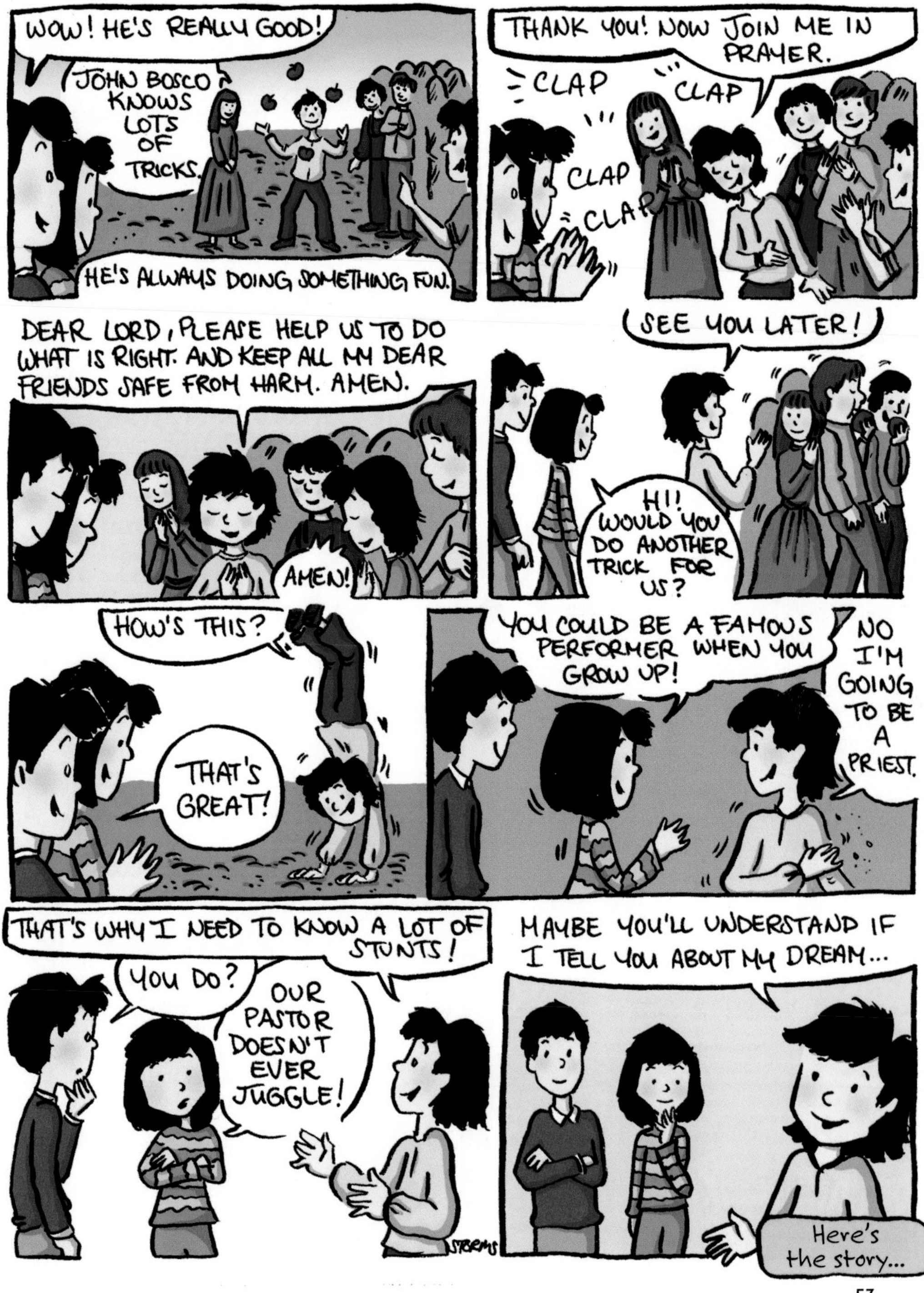
WOW! HE'S REALLY GOOD!
JOHN BOSCO KNOWS LOTS OF TRICKS.
HE'S ALWAYS DOING SOMETHING FUN.
THANK YOU! NOW JOIN ME IN PRAYER.
CLAP
CLAP
CLAP
CLAP
DEAR LORD, PLEASE HELP US TO DO WHAT IS RIGHT. AND KEEP ALL MY DEAR FRIENDS SAFE FROM HARM. AMEN.
AMEN!
SEE YOU LATER!
HI! WOULD YOU DO ANOTHER TRICK FOR US?
HOW'S THIS?
THAT'S GREAT!
YOU COULD BE A FAMOUS PERFORMER WHEN YOU GROW UP!
NO I'M GOING TO BE A PRIEST.
THAT'S WHY I NEED TO KNOW A LOT OF STUNTS!
YOU DO?
OUR PASTOR DOESN'T EVER JUGGLE!
MAYBE YOU'LL UNDERSTAND IF I TELL YOU ABOUT MY DREAM...
Here's the story...

I ALWAYS WANTED TO BRING PEOPLE TO GOD, BUT I WASN'T SURE HOW TO DO THAT.

THEN I HAD A DREAM ABOUT A GROUP OF BOYS PLAYING IN A FIELD. THEY WERE NOT BEHAVING THEMSELVES!

I HIT THEM AND YELLED AT THEM.

STOP USING THAT BAD LANGUAGE! STOP THAT RIGHT NOW! BE GOOD!

THEN THE LORD APPEARED.

JOHN! YOU MUST BECOME THE LEADER OF THESE BOYS.

BUT HOW? THEY WON'T LISTEN TO ME!

THEN I SAW BESIDE HIM A BEAUTIFUL AND MAJESTIC LADY.

LOOK AT THE BOYS NOW, JOHN!

THEY'VE CHANGED! I CAN'T LEAD WILD ANIMALS!

YES, YOU CAN. WHAT HAPPENS TO THESE ANIMALS YOU WILL HAVE TO DO FOR MY CHILDREN. LOOK!

WOW! THEY'RE ALL SWEET AND GENTLE NOW! AND READY TO LISTEN, TOO, I BET!

YOU SEE, THE BOYS DIDN'T LISTEN WHEN I TRIED TO FORCE THEM. I HAD TO USE KINDNESS INSTEAD.

THE DREAM SHOWED ME THAT I COULD BRING CHILDREN TO GOD. WITH KINDNESS! AND SOMETIMES I THROW IN SOMETHING FUN!

ST. JOHN BOSCO MADE HIS DREAM COME TRUE, DIDN'T HE?

YES, HE BECAME A PRIEST AND HELPED MANY POOR CHILDREN.

AND HE LED THEM TO GOD WITHOUT ACTING LIKE THE BOSS OF THE WORLD!

OKAY, OKAY, I GET IT!

I'LL STOP ORDERING PEOPLE AROUND. THEN MAYBE MY FRIENDS WILL WANT TO BE IN MY CLUB.

I'M SURE THEY WILL!

I'M GOING TO TALK TO THEM RIGHT NOW. PUT THE FLUTE AWAY, CECILIA.

IS THAT AN ORDER?

OH, SORRY! WOULD YOU PLEASE PUT THE FLUTE AWAY?

OKAY!

I WONDER IF...

HEY, PAUL! DON'T FORGET TO THROW IN SOMETHING FUN!

But wait... there's more!

55

Don Bosco was followed home one night by two robbers. Suddenly a huge dog appeared and leaped, howling, at the men. They ran! Don Bosco named the dog Grigio ("Gray"). From then on, whenever the priest was in danger, Grigio would appear and save him. Afterward he always slipped away. Was Grigio an ordinary dog . . . or something more? Even Don Bosco never knew for sure.

PRAYER

Saint John, you wanted everyone to grow closer to God. Help me to set a good example for my friends by acting as Jesus would have acted.

John Bosco was born on August 16, 1815, in a small town in the Piedmont region of Italy. His mother, a poor farmer's widow, struggled to keep the family together. John had to work hard as a shepherd to help her. Fortunately, he was able to study with the parish priest, who taught him reading, writing, and religion.

John knew he wanted to become a priest. To pay for his education, he worked as a carpenter, a tailor, and a shoemaker. Finally, in 1841, he was ordained. He became known as Don Bosco (*Don* is an Italian title of respect for a priest).

In the city of Turin, Don Bosco served as a parish priest. One day as he was getting ready for Mass, he heard a commotion. A sacristan, appointed to take care of sacred vessels and vestments, was loudly scolding a ragged boy. "Out! You don't know anything about serving Mass!" he cried.

Don Bosco hurried over. Sending the sacristan away, he asked the boy, "Would you like to learn how to serve?" The grateful boy nodded. The next day, he was back . . . with several friends. Don Bosco soon had many pupils!

Today Salesian priests and sisters operate shelters for homeless youths. They run schools as well as technical, vocational, and language centers.

Some of them were homeless. To help them, he began a school for boys. His mother moved to Turin to assist with the school. The students called her Mamma Margaret.

Soon Don Bosco realized that a new religious congregation was needed to care for and teach the many boys who needed help—not only in his own city, but all over the world. He began the Salesian Society, named after Saint Francis de Sales. Don Bosco's little school became the famous Salesian Oratory. His congregation grew and spread around the globe. In 1888, Don Bosco died, leaving behind a legacy of caring and love.

Saint John Bosco was canonized by one of his greatest admirers, Pope Pius XI, in 1934.

Pray for children around the world who have no homes and no families.

Saint John Bosco

PATRON OF EDITORS, YOUTHS
Feed Day
JANUARY 31

Blessed James Alberione

Do not fear, Mary. You have found favor with God. You shall bear a son and name him Jesus.

How can this be since... oh, my!

CUT!

BAM!!!

Are you hurt, children?

No, Father, we're fine. But we're sorry for interrupting!

And for knocking over the set!

That's all right. We can fix it. Let's take a break!

When we start again, we'll find you a safe place to watch things.

Excuse me, Father Alberione.

When will the set for Mary's visit to Elizabeth need to be ready?

We should get to that scene tomorrow.

This is Elizabeth's costume.

Excellent!

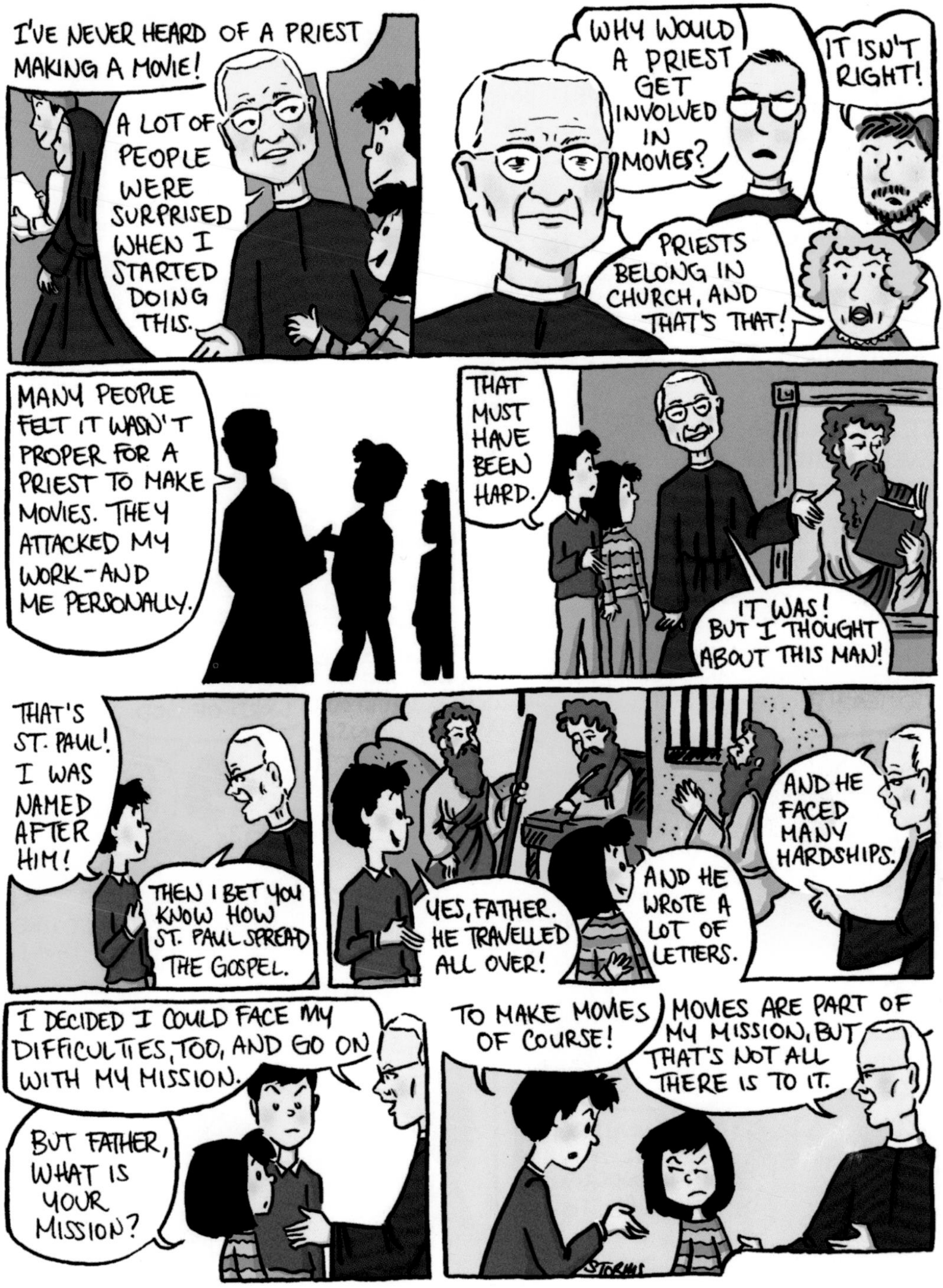
I'VE NEVER HEARD OF A PRIEST MAKING A MOVIE!
A LOT OF PEOPLE WERE SURPRISED WHEN I STARTED DOING THIS.
WHY WOULD A PRIEST GET INVOLVED IN MOVIES?
IT ISN'T RIGHT!
PRIESTS BELONG IN CHURCH, AND THAT'S THAT!
MANY PEOPLE FELT IT WASN'T PROPER FOR A PRIEST TO MAKE MOVIES. THEY ATTACKED MY WORK—AND ME PERSONALLY.
THAT MUST HAVE BEEN HARD.
IT WAS! BUT I THOUGHT ABOUT THIS MAN!
THAT'S ST. PAUL! I WAS NAMED AFTER HIM!
THEN I BET YOU KNOW HOW ST. PAUL SPREAD THE GOSPEL.
YES, FATHER. HE TRAVELLED ALL OVER!
AND HE WROTE A LOT OF LETTERS.
AND HE FACED MANY HARDSHIPS.
I DECIDED I COULD FACE MY DIFFICULTIES, TOO, AND GO ON WITH MY MISSION.
BUT FATHER, WHAT IS YOUR MISSION?
TO MAKE MOVIES OF COURSE!
MOVIES ARE PART OF MY MISSION, BUT THAT'S NOT ALL THERE IS TO IT.
STORMS

A NEW CENTURY IS STARTING, LORD. HOW CAN I SERVE YOU?

I CAN SPREAD THE GOSPEL TO THE WORLD! LIKE ST. PAUL, I'LL USE EVERY METHOD OF COMMUNICATION THAT I CAN.

I WAS JUST A YOUNG MAN THEN, STUDYING FOR THE PRIESTHOOD. BUT FROM THAT NIGHT ON, MY MISSION WAS CLEAR.

WITH THE HELP OF MANY GOOD PEOPLE, I PUBLISH BOOKS AND MAGAZINES TO TEACH PEOPLE ABOUT JESUS.

WOW!

WE REACH PEOPLE AROUND THE WORLD WITH OUR PUBLICATIONS.

La Primera Biblia para el niño

Testimonio Dello Spirito

AND MY FOLLOWERS TRAVEL ALL OVER TO SPREAD THE WORD OF GOD.

JUST LIKE ST. PAUL!

OOPS! SORRY, FATHER. I JUST WANTED TO READ ONE.

CRASH!

HE LO-O-O-OVES READING!

READING IS A WONDERFUL WAY TO LEARN!

BUT I WANTED TO COMMUNICATE JESUS TO AS MANY PEOPLE AS I COULD, SO I STARTED MAKING MOVIES.

DO YOU LIKE MOVIES, TOO, CHILDREN?

YE-ES, BUT MOM WANTS TO KNOW ABOUT WHAT WE SEE.

AND WHAT WE READ.

I'M NOT SURE ABOUT SOME OF THE THINGS MY FRIENDS READ AND WATCH.

WHEN I SEE A MOVIE, MOM AND I TALK ABOUT IT.

THAT'S A GREAT IDEA. NOT ALL MOVIES ARE APPROPRIATE FOR CHILDREN YOUR AGE, BUT REMEMBER THAT THERE ARE GOOD MOVIES AND WORTHWHILE THINGS TO READ, TOO.

AND THEY CAN HAVE A POWERFUL AND POSITIVE INFLUENCE ON PEOPLE'S LIVES!

WHO KNOWS? MAYBE SOMEDAY THERE WILL BE NEW WAYS TO SPREAD THE WORD OF GOD.

THE MUSIC!

SO SOON?

I BET FATHER ALBERIONE DIDN'T KNOW ABOUT COMPUTERS AND THE INTERNET BACK THEN!

BUT HIS FOLLOWERS STILL USE ALL THE NEW TECHNOLOGIES TO COMMUNICATE THE GOSPEL.

MAYBE WHEN I GROW UP, I'LL MAKE MOVIES LIKE FATHER ALBERIONE DID. HEY! YOU COULD BE AN AUTHOR!

MAYBE.

I'M GOING TO SEE IF MOM AND DAD WILL LET ME USE THE VIDEO CAMERA.

MAYBE I COULD DO IT!

A GOOD BOOK BY PAUL YOUNG

But wait... there's more!

STORMS

"Prayer first of all,

Feast Day
NOVEMBER 26

Pray that writers, filmmakers, actors, video game designers, and musicians will use media to spread positive messages.

Blessed James Alberione

Blessed James Alberione was the founder of the Pauline family. Today over 10,000 members worldwide belong to its ten religious congregations and secular institutes.

In 1884, a son was born to Teresa and Michael Alberione, farmers in a small northern Italian town. Little James was frail and sickly. As he grew older, though, he became stronger. He also grew in his faith and love for God.

By the age of six, James had decided to become a priest. When he was twelve, he began attending school in Turin. Although James was a good student, things started to change when he was sixteen. He went through a difficult time, and soon the headmaster decided to send James home. James was shocked. He still wanted to become a priest…but how?

prayer above all, prayer the life of all."

Father James was declared "blessed" by Pope John Paul II in 2003. Mother Thecla Merlo was declared "venerable" by the Church in 1991.

After six months of hard work, James was accepted at the seminary in Alba. He spent the night between December 31, 1900 and January 1, 1901 at midnight Mass. Afterward James prayed for hours. He felt a light coming to him from Jesus in the Blessed Sacrament. God was calling him to bring the Gospel to as many people as possible. James knew that Jesus would show him the way.

Five years later, James was ordained a priest. Soon he realized he was called to begin a new religious congregation to bring Jesus' Word to the world. In 1914 he opened a printing shop with two students as helpers. This was the beginning of the Society of St. Paul, which uses modern media to communicate the message of Jesus around the globe.

In June 1915, with the help of a young woman named Teresa Merlo, Father James began a congregation of women religious to aid in the mission. When Teresa made her vows, she took the name Thecla, one of the original helpers of Saint Paul. The congregation is called the Daughters of St. Paul.

After a long life of prayer and work, Father James Alberione died on November 26, 1971.

The first Paulines who worked with Father James learned to print books and magazines, run radio stations, and make movies! From the early twentieth century through the present day, the Paulines have established congregations in countries around the world. These men and women have shared the Good News through media in many different languages and cultures.

PRAYER

Blessed James, today we have so many kinds of media—television, movies, the Internet, video games, and so much more. Please help me to use media wisely and responsibly.

Saint Juan Diego

WE WON! THANKS TO ME! I SCORED THE WINNING GOAL!

HEY, I CAME UP HERE TO DO MY BIBLE STUDY.

YOU SHOULD HAVE SEEN ME, CECILIA. I WAS WEAVING DOWN THE FIELD AND—

AND YOU WERE A BIG STAR! I KNOW!

WHAT'S YOUR PROBLEM?

YOU'RE ALWAYS BRAGGING ABOUT SOCCER. I THINK YOUR HEAD IS GETTING BIGGER THAN THAT BALL!

HUH?

OH IT IS NOT! ANYWAY, IT'S NOT BRAGGING WHEN YOU REALLY ARE A STAR!

WHATEVER. LET'S TRY THIS NEW MUSIC.

THANK YOU FOR TELLING US YOUR STORY, JUAN DIEGO.

YOU ARE AN INSPIRATION!

ME? NO, IT'S OUR MOTHER MARY WHO IS THE INSPIRATION.

HAVE A SAFE JOURNEY HOME.

GOOD-BYE! THANK YOU!

COULD WE HEAR YOUR STORY, TOO?

OF COURSE, CHILDREN! THAT'S WHY I'M HERE.

WHEN THIS CHURCH WAS BUILT, I BECAME THE CARETAKER. SO I'M ALWAYS AROUND TO SHARE MY JOYOUS STORY.

I USED TO WALK FIFTEEN MILES TO A CHURCH. NOW I LIVE RIGHT NEXT DOOR!

A POOR MAN LIKE ME!

FIFTEEN MILES? WOW!

YEAH... WOW... UH... WAS THAT THE WHOLE STORY?

NO! BUT MY STORY BEGINS WITH ONE OF THOSE LONG WALKS. SEE, I WAS GOING TO CHURCH ONE WINTER DAY...

... AND I HEARD SOMETHING.

LITTLE JUAN! LITTLE JUAN!

IT MUST BE SOMEONE I KNOW. I'LL GO UP AND SEE WHO IT IS.

THEN I EXPERIENCED SOMETHING AMAZING!

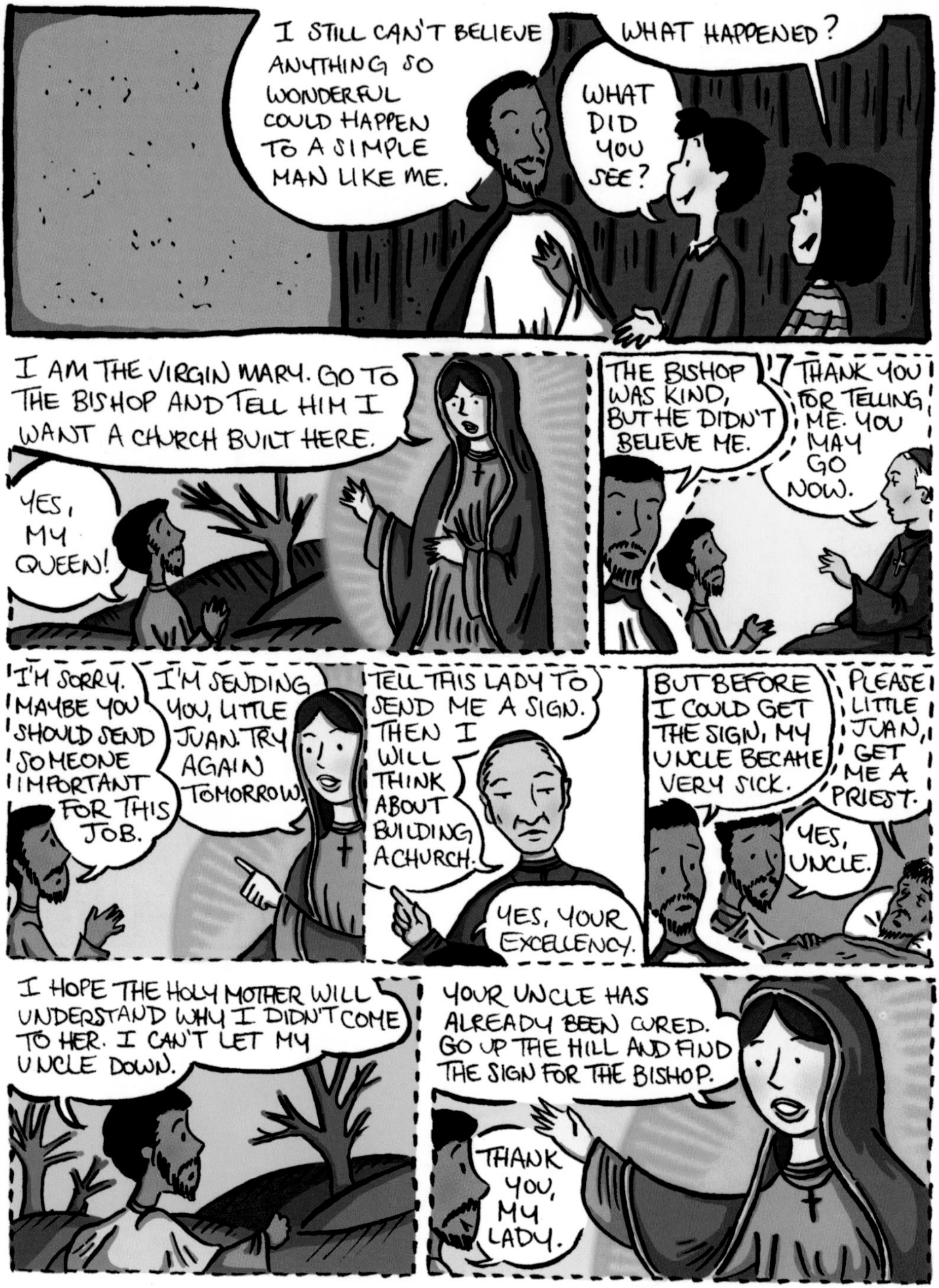

I STILL CAN'T BELIEVE ANYTHING SO WONDERFUL COULD HAPPEN TO A SIMPLE MAN LIKE ME.
WHAT HAPPENED?
WHAT DID YOU SEE?
I AM THE VIRGIN MARY. GO TO THE BISHOP AND TELL HIM I WANT A CHURCH BUILT HERE.
YES, MY QUEEN!
THE BISHOP WAS KIND, BUT HE DIDN'T BELIEVE ME.
THANK YOU FOR TELLING ME. YOU MAY GO NOW.
I'M SORRY. MAYBE YOU SHOULD SEND SOMEONE IMPORTANT FOR THIS JOB.
I'M SENDING YOU, LITTLE JUAN. TRY AGAIN TOMORROW.
TELL THIS LADY TO SEND ME A SIGN. THEN I WILL THINK ABOUT BUILDING A CHURCH.
YES, YOUR EXCELLENCY.
BUT BEFORE I COULD GET THE SIGN, MY UNCLE BECAME VERY SICK.
PLEASE LITTLE JUAN, GET ME A PRIEST.
YES, UNCLE.
I HOPE THE HOLY MOTHER WILL UNDERSTAND WHY I DIDN'T COME TO HER. I CAN'T LET MY UNCLE DOWN.
YOUR UNCLE HAS ALREADY BEEN CURED. GO UP THE HILL AND FIND THE SIGN FOR THE BISHOP.
THANK YOU, MY LADY.

I'VE NEVER SEEN SUCH BEAUTIFUL FLOWERS! AND IN THE WINTERTIME! I'LL PICK SOME AND CARRY THEM IN MY CLOAK.

I TOOK THE FLOWERS TO THE BISHOP.

MY LADY HAS SENT YOU THIS SIGN.

ROSES? WHY THAT'S ASTOUNDING!

IT'S A MIRACLE! WE WILL BUILD THE CHURCH. AND WE'LL DISPLAY THIS CLOAK INSIDE.

A PICTURE OF THE HOLY MOTHER ON MY OLD CLOAK! WHAT A BLESSING AND A GIFT FROM GOD!

THE MUSIC!

WOW! THE MOTHER OF GOD CAME TO JUAN DIEGO, BUT HE WAS STILL SO... I DON'T KNOW...

HUMBLE?

HE SURE WAS. INSTEAD OF BRAGGING ABOUT HIS AMAZING EXPERIENCE, HE WAS GRATEFUL THAT IT HAPPENED TO HIM.

I'M SORRY I MADE A BIG DEAL ABOUT MYSELF BEFORE I'M GOING TO TRY TO BE MORE LIKE ST. JUAN DIEGO.

HMMM... IS YOUR HEAD SHRINKING?

FUNNY! GIVE ME THAT BALL.

CATCH ME IF YOU CAN!

COME BACK HERE!

But wait...there's more!

"I am unworthy, but I will try my best."

Pray for the farmers and migrant workers of Mexico.

By his bishop's special ruling, Juan Diego was permitted to receive Holy Communion three times a week, an unusual occurrence in those days. Pope John Paul II canonized him in 2002.

In 1474, a son was born to Aztec parents. He was called Cuauhtlatoatzin, or "talking eagle." When the boy grew up, he became a farmer. Cuauhtlatoatzin learned about Jesus when Franciscan friars from Spain arrived in the 1520s. At the age of fifty, he was baptized. His baptismal name was Juan Diego.

Christopher Columbus had arrived in the New World only thirty-nine years before the Blessed Mother appeared to Juan Diego on a hill called Tepeyac. Some of the native people of the land we call Mexico were eager, like Juan Diego, to learn about Jesus and to receive Baptism. Many, however, were suspicious of the Christian friars.

Feast Day
December 9

Saint Juan Diego

The *conquistadors* (armies of conquerors) sent by the Spanish king were often cruel and unfair to the native people. They stole their riches, destroyed their cities, and even killed them for their gold. Bishop Zumárraga and his fellow priests were saddened and frustrated by this behavior. How could they convince the native people that Jesus is our Savior? The bishop prayed for a sign from heaven.

And he got one! When Juan Diego brought him the news of Mary's appearance, the bishop was astonished to see lovely roses sent by the Blessed Mother. They were a type of Spanish rose that didn't grow in the New World. Only a miracle could have made them appear!

He was also astonished by the image of Mary found on Juan Diego's *tilma*, a coarse cloth woven from cactus fibers. The bishop understood then why Mary had asked Juan Diego for a chapel to be built, for many native people would come to Jesus because of these signs from heaven.

"The chapel will be built," promised the bishop. And when it was, the *tilma* was displayed for all to see!

Although *tilma* fabric usually falls apart within twenty years, the miraculous *tilma* of Saint Juan Diego is still displayed at the new Basilica of Our Lady of Guadalupe, which was completed in 1976. It shows a pregnant woman with Aztec features and clothing. Her blue cloak is covered with golden stars, and she stands on an image of the moon.

Within seven years after Our Lady of Guadalupe's visits to Juan Diego, more than 8 million native Mexicans were converted to the Catholic faith.

PRAYER

Saint Juan Diego, you were determined to deliver Mary's message, even when you weren't believed. Help me to be as faithful and committed as you were.

Saint Elizabeth of Hungary

LIKE I'M GOING TO DO THIS!

CRUMPLE!!!

IF YOU'RE GOING TO THROW THINGS, THEN YOU NEED TO AIM BETTER.

WHATEVER.

WHY ARE YOU IN SUCH A BAD MOOD? OH. IT'S THE FLYER ABOUT THE FOOD DRIVE.

YEAH. THAT'S A GREAT IDEA FOR THE REST OF YOUTH GROUP, BUT NOT FOR US.

REALLY! WE HAVE OUR OWN PROBLEMS.

I WISH DAD'S NEW JOB PAID BETTER.

MAYBE THEN WE COULD AFFORD TO HELP WITH THE FOOD DRIVE.

AND THE CHRISTMAS TOY DRIVE, TOO. I'D LIKE TO HELP NEEDY PEOPLE, BUT WE'VE ALREADY SACRIFICED ENOUGH.

I AGREE!

AT LEAST OUR TRAVELS WITH THE FLUTE ARE FREE!

IS THIS SOME KIND OF HOSPITAL?

IT DOES LOOK LIKE A PLACE FOR SICK PEOPLE. LET'S GO INSIDE.

HERE YOU GO. DRINK SLOWLY NOW.

ELIZABETH ALWAYS WORKS WITH THE SICKEST PATIENTS.

I KNOW! HOW KIND SHE IS!

I WONDER WHERE THE NICE LADY IS GOING NOW.

LET'S FOLLOW HER AND SEE.

SHE'S GIVING THE POOR PEOPLE SOMETHING TO EAT.

WOW! SHE REALLY IS KIND.

THANK YOU, YOUR HIGHNESS.

YOUR HIGHNESS?

STORES

71

ARE YOU REALLY A PRINCESS?

HE HAS? BUT SHOULDN'T YOU HAVE FANCY CLOTHES?

YES, I AM. GOD HAS TRULY BLESSED ME.

AND WHY AREN'T YOU TAKING IT EASY IN YOUR CASTLE?

LET ME EXPLAIN MY BLESSINGS TO YOU.

EVEN THOUGH MY PARENTS ARRANGED MY ENGAGEMENT, I HAD A HAPPY MARRIAGE. MY HUSBAND WAS SUCH A GOOD MAN!

WE LIVED IN A LOVELY CASTLE WITH EVERY— THING I COULD WANT.

GOD HAS GIVEN US ANOTHER BEAUTIFUL CHILD!

THANK THE LORD!

IT SOUNDS WONDERFUL!

AND DO YOU KNOW WHAT WAS THE GREATEST BLESSING OF ALL?

I CAN'T GUESS!

GOD MADE IT POSSIBLE FOR ME TO HELP THE SICK AND POOR! I HAD PLENTY OF MONEY AND CLOTHES TO GIVE AWAY.

I THINK THIS DRESS WILL FIT YOU.

OH THANK YOU! IT'S BEAUTIFUL!

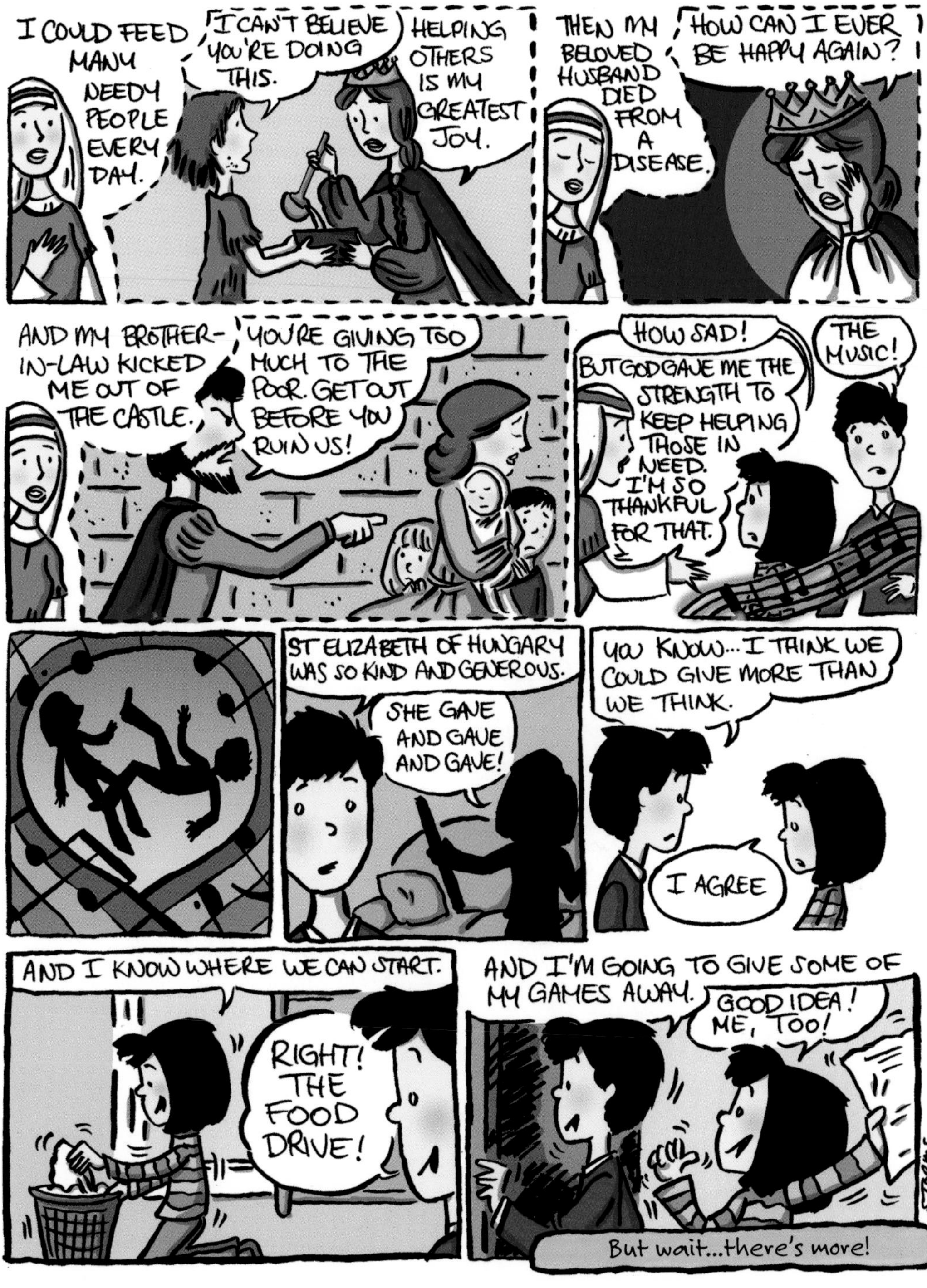
I COULD FEED MANY NEEDY PEOPLE EVERY DAY.
I CAN'T BELIEVE YOU'RE DOING THIS.
HELPING OTHERS IS MY GREATEST JOY.
THEN MY BELOVED HUSBAND DIED FROM A DISEASE.
HOW CAN I EVER BE HAPPY AGAIN?
AND MY BROTHER-IN-LAW KICKED ME OUT OF THE CASTLE.
YOU'RE GIVING TOO MUCH TO THE POOR. GET OUT BEFORE YOU RUIN US!
HOW SAD!
BUT GOD GAVE ME THE STRENGTH TO KEEP HELPING THOSE IN NEED. I'M SO THANKFUL FOR THAT.
THE MUSIC!
ST ELIZABETH OF HUNGARY WAS SO KIND AND GENEROUS.
SHE GAVE AND GAVE AND GAVE!
YOU KNOW... I THINK WE COULD GIVE MORE THAN WE THINK.
I AGREE
AND I KNOW WHERE WE CAN START.
RIGHT! THE FOOD DRIVE!
AND I'M GOING TO GIVE SOME OF MY GAMES AWAY.
GOOD IDEA! ME, TOO!
STORMS
But wait...there's more!

"We each must make ourself the neighbor

One of the most famous legends about Saint Elizabeth tells of her errand of mercy to a sick woman. Elizabeth carried a loaf of bread under her cloak as she left the castle. Ludwig asked where she was going. She told him and opened the cloak to show him the bread . . . but instead her cloak was filled with fragrant roses!

Saint Elizabeth, no matter how little I may have, help me to find a way to share my blessings with others.

Elizabeth, the daughter of King Andrew and Queen Gertrude, was born in Presburg, Hungary, in 1207. In those days, it was usual for royal families to plan marriages for their children at a very young age. When Elizabeth was only four years old, she was betrothed, or engaged, to Ludwig, the oldest son of the Duke of Thuringia in central Germany. She was sent to live with the duke's family until both children would be old enough to wed.

When Elizabeth was fourteen, she and Ludwig were married. Marriage at that age was quite common in those times, although it seems very young to us now! Their marriage was a happy one, and they had three children.

Soon Franciscan friars arrived in Thuringia, and Elizabeth began to learn about the ideals of Francis of Assisi. Brother Francis was known for his kindness to the poor and his care for all of God's creation. Elizabeth decided that she, too, wanted to live Jesus' teachings. She became known for her charitable activities, giving alms to the poor and starting a hospital near the castle.

In 1227, Ludwig died of the plague, a terrible disease in those days. His brother

Many parish churches in the United States and Canada are named for this beloved saint.

of everyone."

was furious that Elizabeth continued to give so much to the poor. "You'll bankrupt us!" he declared. Elizabeth and her children were forced to leave the castle. After a period of homelessness, she was received by her family and was able to recover enough money from her husband's family to live on.

She became one of the first *tertiaries* (secular, meaning she was not a nun), members of the Franciscan Third Order in Germany. For the rest of her short life, Elizabeth worked to help the poor, establishing meal centers and hospitals and giving tirelessly to those who needed her help. She was twenty-four when she died in 1231.

PATRON OF HOSPITALS,
MEAL CENTERS, BAKERS
Feast Day
NOVEMBER 17

Pray for all people who are living in homeless shelters or on the streets.

Like Elizabeth, Ludwig was pious and kind. In Germany he is honored as "Saint Ludwig," although he was never canonized by the Church. Elizabeth was canonized by Pope Gregory IX in 1235.

Saint Elizabeth of Hungary

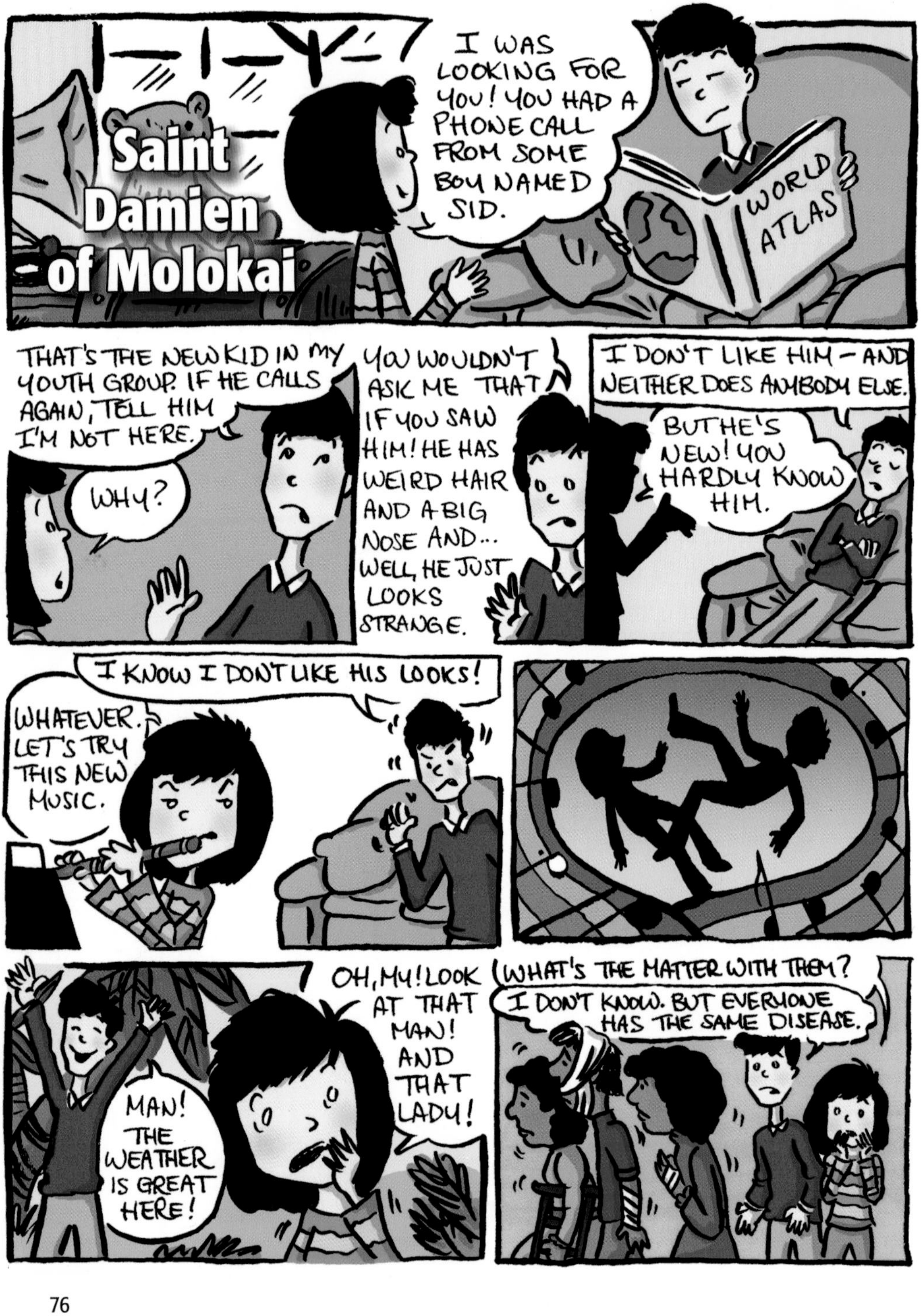
Saint Damien of Molokai
I WAS LOOKING FOR YOU! YOU HAD A PHONE CALL FROM SOME BOY NAMED SID.
WORLD ATLAS
THAT'S THE NEW KID IN MY YOUTH GROUP. IF HE CALLS AGAIN, TELL HIM I'M NOT HERE.
WHY?
YOU WOULDN'T ASK ME THAT IF YOU SAW HIM! HE HAS WEIRD HAIR AND A BIG NOSE AND... WELL, HE JUST LOOKS STRANGE.
I DON'T LIKE HIM – AND NEITHER DOES ANYBODY ELSE.
BUT HE'S NEW! YOU HARDLY KNOW HIM.
I KNOW I DON'T LIKE HIS LOOKS!
WHATEVER. LET'S TRY THIS NEW MUSIC.
MAN! THE WEATHER IS GREAT HERE!
OH, MY! LOOK AT THAT MAN! AND THAT LADY!
WHAT'S THE MATTER WITH THEM?
I DON'T KNOW. BUT EVERYONE HAS THE SAME DISEASE.

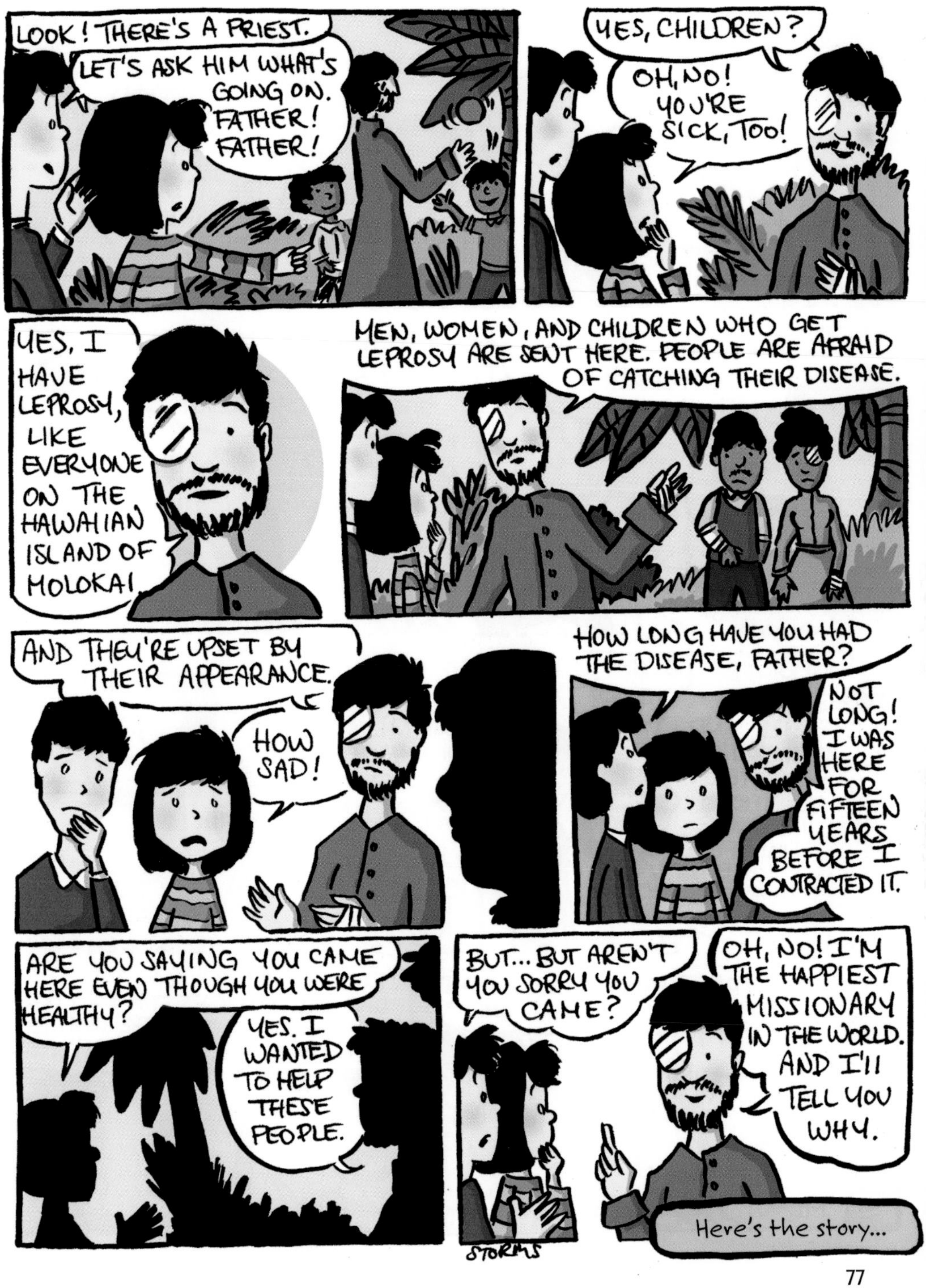

LOOK! THERE'S A PRIEST.
LET'S ASK HIM WHAT'S GOING ON. FATHER! FATHER!
YES, CHILDREN?
OH, NO! YOU'RE SICK, TOO!
YES, I HAVE LEPROSY, LIKE EVERYONE ON THE HAWAIIAN ISLAND OF MOLOKAI.
MEN, WOMEN, AND CHILDREN WHO GET LEPROSY ARE SENT HERE. PEOPLE ARE AFRAID OF CATCHING THEIR DISEASE.
AND THEY'RE UPSET BY THEIR APPEARANCE.
HOW SAD!
HOW LONG HAVE YOU HAD THE DISEASE, FATHER?
NOT LONG! I WAS HERE FOR FIFTEEN YEARS BEFORE I CONTRACTED IT.
ARE YOU SAYING YOU CAME HERE EVEN THOUGH YOU WERE HEALTHY?
YES. I WANTED TO HELP THESE PEOPLE.
BUT... BUT AREN'T YOU SORRY YOU CAME?
OH, NO! I'M THE HAPPIEST MISSIONARY IN THE WORLD. AND I'll TELL YOU WHY.
Here's the story...
STORMS

THESE HUTS ARE FALLING APART.

WHEN I CAME TO MOLOKAI, I WAS SHOCKED. AND NOT JUST BY THE WAY THE PEOPLE LOOKED.

AND THIS HOSPITAL IS IN TERRIBLE SHAPE!

I MUST HELP THESE PEOPLE. THEY ARE SICK, BUT THEY ARE GOD'S CHILDREN!

I PRAYED WITH THE PEOPLE AND BROUGHT THE SACRAMENT TO THEM. THAT MADE THEM FEEL MORE HOPEFUL.

I BET IT DID!

WE FIXED UP THE HOUSES AND THE HOSPITAL. AND WE BUILT AN ORPHANAGE. TOGETHER WE WORKED TO MAKE MOLOKAI A BETTER PLACE.

BUT ISN'T IT HARD... I MEAN... BEING AROUND PEOPLE WHO LOOK LIKE THAT?

PAUL!

IT'S ALL RIGHT. I UNDERSTAND WHAT YOU MEAN.

THINK OF IT THIS WAY. THE DISEASE DAMAGES THE BODY, BUT NOT THE SOUL WITHIN. THE PEOPLE OF MOLOKOI ARE WONDERFUL PEOPLE!

THEY DEAL WITH TERRIBLE DIFFICULTIES EVERY DAY, AND THEY DO SO WITH GREAT COURAGE AND LOVE.

I FEEL BLESSED TO HAVE KNOWN THESE PEOPLE! AND I AM HAPPY NOW TO BE TRULY ONE OF THEM.

FATHER DAMIEN!

THE MUSIC!

PLAY WITH US!

I'M COMING!

FATHER DAMIEN HAD SUCH A BIG HEART.

YES, HE DID. BACK THEN THERE WAS NO CURE FOR LEPROSY. NOW IT'S CALLED HANSEN'S DISEASE, AND THERE ARE MEDICINES TO CURE IT.

FATHER DAMIEN REALLY CARED ABOUT HIS PEOPLE, IN SPITE OF THEIR DISEASE.

YEAH. HE TREATED THEM KINDLY.

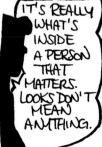

IT'S REALLY WHAT'S INSIDE A PERSON THAT MATTERS. LOOKS DON'T MEAN ANYTHING.

DO YOU REALLY BELIEVE THAT?

YES! AND I'M GOING TO GIVE SID A CHANCE.

I WROTE HIS NUMBER ON THE PAD BY THE PHONE.

THANKS! I'M GOING TO CALL HIM RIGHT NOW.

GOOD IDEA!

But wait...there's more!

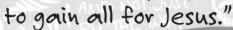

"I make myself a leper with the lepers, to gain all for Jesus."

Pray for people with leprosy (now called Hansen's disease) in developing countries, where medicines may not be available.

Saint Damien of Molokai

Saint Damien is revered in Hawaii. The state has honored his memory with a statue that stands in the Rotunda of the U.S. Capitol in Washington, D.C.

Joseph de Veuster was born in 1840 into a farm family in Belgium. When they grew up, Joseph and his brother, Pamphile, joined the missionary Congregation of the Sacred Hearts of Jesus and Mary. Joseph chose the religious name Damien.

While Damien was still studying to become a priest, his brother was assigned as a missionary to bring Christianity to the Hawaiian people. Pamphile became ill, and Damien quickly volunteered to take his place. Two months after arriving, Damien was ordained a priest in Honolulu.

After nine years of serving on the Big Island of Hawaii, Father Damien heard about a major problem. A disease

PATRON OF HAWAII, PEOPLE WITH HANSEN'S DISEASE, THOSE LIVING WITH HIV/AIDS
Feast Day MAY 10

called leprosy had been brought to the islands by settlers and sailors. Some Hawaiian people had caught leprosy. The government was worried. What if this serious disease spread even more? In 1866, it was decreed that everyone with leprosy would be moved to live on an isolated part of the island of Molokai. Unfortunately, the sufferers had no dwellings, few provisions, and no doctors or priests. They lived miserably, forgotten by the rest of society. When Father Damien heard about their sad plight, he knew he had to help.

In 1873, Father Damien sailed to Molokai. He got right to work cleaning wounds and bandaging arms and legs damaged by the disease. He organized the settlers into work teams. When a hurricane destroyed the flimsy huts of the settlement, he asked the government to send lumber and supplies to build 300 new houses. He even dug and laid a pipeline for fresh water. In his spare time, Father Damien formed a choir and a band!

After twelve years on Molokai, Father Damien became ill with leprosy himself. He continued to work tirelessly until his death in 1889.

Hawaii was settled by Polynesians between 300 and 600 A.D. In Father Damien's time, Hawaii was ruled by King Kamehameha V. The Molokai orchestra became famous when it performed a Mozart Mass for Queen Liliuokalani, the last queen of Hawaii, in 1881. Hawaii became a U.S. territory in 1900 and a state in 1959.

PRAYER

Saint Damien, you put the welfare of others before your own needs. Help me to be as unselfish and caring as you were.

Saint Thérèse of Lisieux

ARE YOU ASLEEP?

YES.

FUNNY. WHY ARE YOU SLEEPING IN THE MIDDLE OF THE AFTERNOON?

I'M TIRED. DAD AND I PAINTED THE WHOLE GARAGE!

I KNOW! I WANTED TO HELP, BUT MOM AND DAD SAID I'M TOO YOUNG. THEY NEVER LET ME DO ANYTHING IMPORTANT.

WHAT ABOUT YOUR CHORES?

THOSE ARE JUST LITTLE JOBS! YOU GET TO DO BIG THINGS LIKE PAINT AND BUILD THE NEW FENCE.

HERE'S A JOB FOR YOU! PLAY THE NEW MUSIC.

OH, OKAY.

YOU'RE GOING TOO SLOWLY. I'M NOT AN INVALID, YOU KNOW.

I'M SORRY, SISTER.

NOW YOU'RE GOING TOO FAST. YOU'LL MAKE ME FALL!

FORGIVE ME, SISTER. I'LL SLOW DOWN.

OUCH! GOODNESS, SISTER THÉRÈSE! MUST YOU ALWAYS BE SO ROUGH?

I'M SORRY, SISTER. THANK YOU FOR BEING SO PATIENT WITH ME.

BONJOUR, CHILDREN.

THAT MEANS 'GOOD DAY'.

OH. BONJOUR, SISTER. BUT IT DOESN'T LOOK LIKE YOU'RE HAVING A GOOD DAY.

I'M HAVING A WONDERFUL DAY. AND NOW IT'S GOING TO GET EVEN BETTER.

HOW COULD IT GET WORSE?

REALLY!

SO... YOU... UM... MUST REALLY LIKE DOING YOUR CHORES.

OH, GOODNESS NO! BUT I LOVE JESUS SO MUCH.

AND IT GIVES ME GREAT JOY TO SHOW HIM MY LOVE. HERE'S ANOTHER CHANCE TO DO THAT WITH THESE CLOAKS.

WE DON'T UNDERSTAND, SISTER.

WHAT DO THESE LITTLE JOBS HAVE TO DO WITH JESUS?

I'LL TRY TO EXPLAIN IT TO YOU.

STORMS

I KNEW I WANTED TO ENTER THIS CONVENT WHEN I WAS A CHILD, BUT EVERYONE SAID I WAS TOO YOUNG.

HOW UNFAIR!

NO, I WASN'T READY. BUT WHEN GOD DECIDED I WAS, I CAME HERE TO LIVE A LIFE DEVOTED TO HIM.

I WAS HAPPY, BUT I HAD A WISH IN MY HEART.

IF ONLY I COULD DO GREAT DEEDS FOR YOU, LORD!

BUT HOW COULD A LITTLE BIRD LIKE ME DO SOMETHING GLORIOUS? WHEN YOU CAN'T DO ANYTHING IMPORTANT, YOU'RE NOBODY, RIGHT?

NOT AT ALL! JESUS USED THE BEAUTY OF NATURE TO TEACH ME THAT'S NOT TRUE. IT HAPPENED IN THE GARDEN...

AREN'T THESE LITTLE VIOLETS LOVELY? THEY DON'T HAVE THE SPLENDOR OF THE ROSES AND LILIES, BUT GOD MADE THEM BEAUTIFUL, TOO!

I UNDERSTOOD THEN THAT THERE ARE MANY DIFFERENT SOULS IN JESUS' GARDEN. AND HE LOVES US ALL, GREAT AND SMALL!

JESUS DOESN'T DEMAND HEROIC ACTIONS FROM EVERYONE. HE JUST WANTS US TO LIVE OUR LIVES WITH LOVE.

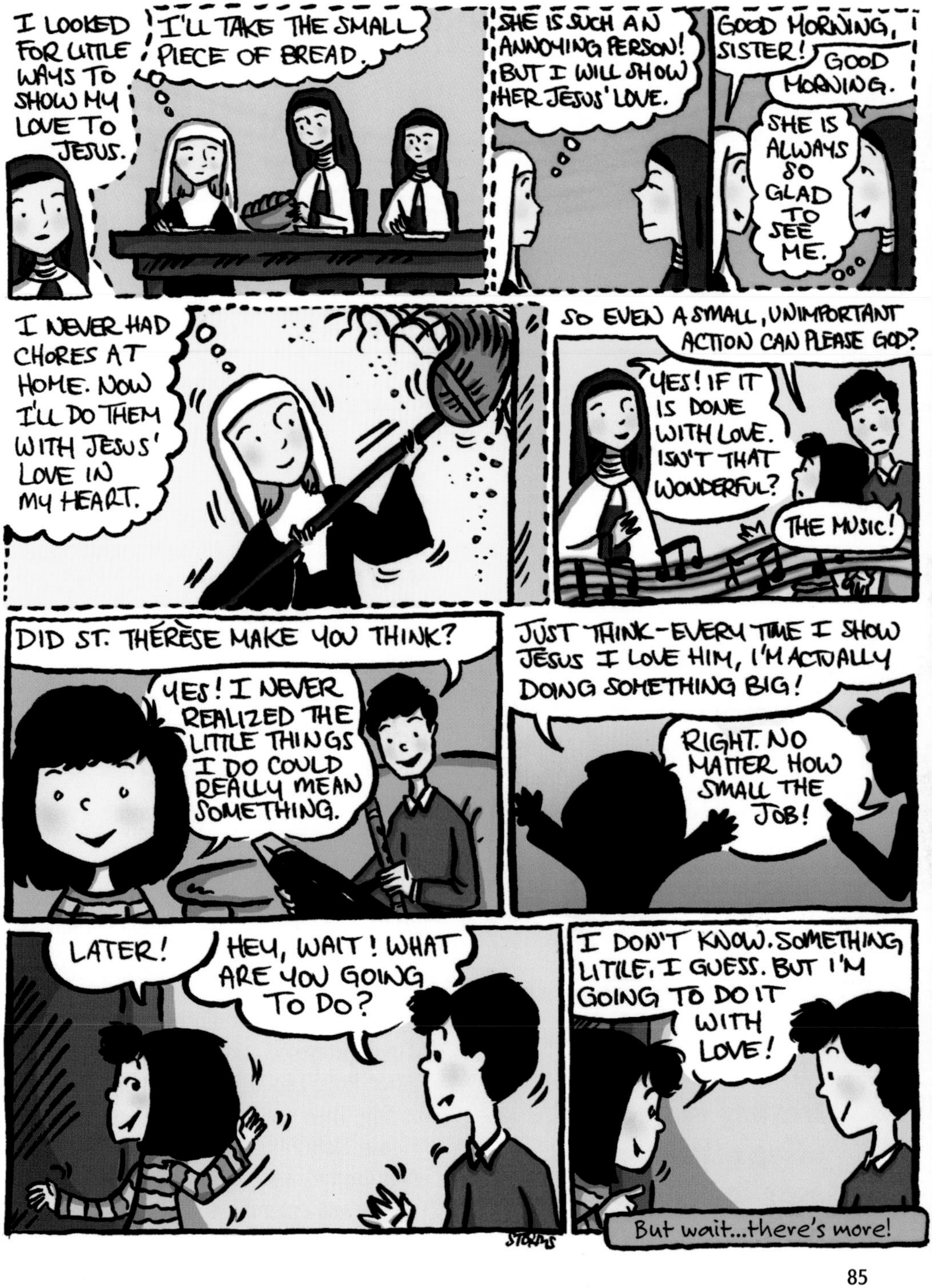
I LOOKED FOR LITTLE WAYS TO SHOW MY LOVE TO JESUS.
I'LL TAKE THE SMALL PIECE OF BREAD.
SHE IS SUCH AN ANNOYING PERSON! BUT I WILL SHOW HER JESUS' LOVE.
GOOD MORNING, SISTER!
GOOD MORNING.
SHE IS ALWAYS SO GLAD TO SEE ME.
I NEVER HAD CHORES AT HOME. NOW I'LL DO THEM WITH JESUS' LOVE IN MY HEART.
SO EVEN A SMALL, UNIMPORTANT ACTION CAN PLEASE GOD?
YES! IF IT IS DONE WITH LOVE. ISN'T THAT WONDERFUL?
THE MUSIC!
DID ST. THÉRÈSE MAKE YOU THINK?
YES! I NEVER REALIZED THE LITTLE THINGS I DO COULD REALLY MEAN SOMETHING.
JUST THINK—EVERY TIME I SHOW JESUS I LOVE HIM, I'M ACTUALLY DOING SOMETHING BIG!
RIGHT. NO MATTER HOW SMALL THE JOB!
LATER!
HEY, WAIT! WHAT ARE YOU GOING TO DO?
I DON'T KNOW. SOMETHING LITTLE, I GUESS. BUT I'M GOING TO DO IT WITH LOVE!
STORMS
But wait...there's more!

"I accept all for love of the good God."

Carmelite nuns are cloistered. That means they spend their days, and even parts of their nights, in prayer and meditation. They generally don't leave their monastery, and they receive visitors only in certain areas of the building at designated times.

Saint Thérèse, help me to cheerfully live your "little way" of love by treating everyone kindly, being patient, and accepting things that are hard.

PATRON OF FRANCE, MISSIONARIES, TUBERCULOSIS PATIENTS
Feast Day
OCTOBER 1

Thérèse Martin was born in Alençon, France, on January 2, 1873. The youngest of five girls, Thérèse was only five when her mother died. Her older sisters Pauline and Marie took special care of her. Thérèse was devoted to Jesus. When Pauline left home to enter a Carmelite monastery, ten-year-old Thérèse knew that someday she, too, would enter Carmel.

By the time she was fourteen, Thérèse had asked permission to enter the order—and been turned down. "Not until you're twenty-one," she was told. But the young girl wasn't giving up!

Soon after, the Martin family joined a pilgrimage from their diocese to Rome. At their promised audience with the Holy Father, Pope Leo XIII, she knelt and kissed his ring. Then she made her request: "Please, Holy Father, will you allow me to enter Carmel, although I'm just fifteen?"

"You will enter if it is God's will," the Pope promised her.

And the Pope was right! Thérèse was allowed to enter the Carmelite Order on April 9, 1888. Her religious name was Sister Thérèse of the Child Jesus.

Sister Thérèse asked God's help in doing each duty, even the smallest and least important, in the best way possible. Her famous "little way" to God was made up of prayer, humility, and love. Whether it was time to sweep the kitchen, pray, or help care for a sick sister, Thérèse did it as if it were the most important thing in the world.

Eventually Sister Thérèse became ill. When a doctor examined her, he found she had a serious form of tuberculosis, a lung disease. At that time there was no medicine that could help her. She died in 1897 at the age of twenty-four.

Saint Thérèse of Lisieux

Pray for people around the world who suffer from serious diseases, especially tuberculosis and HIV/AIDS.

Thérèse couldn't imagine who would want to read her autobiography, but when asked to write it, she obeyed. Today *Story of a Soul* has been translated into dozens of languages all over the world.

Saint Moses the Black

NOW LOOK WHAT YOU DID! I TOLD YOU NOT TO PLAY THE FLUTE. I WAS RIGHT IN THE MIDDLE OF SOMETHING!

YOU WERE JUST PLAYING A GAME!

I WAS ALMOST TO THE NEXT LEVEL. YOU RUINED EVERYTHING!

WHAT KIND OF A PERSON ARE YOU? YOU CARE MORE ABOUT A GAME THAN YOUR FAITH. I WANT TO LEARN ABOUT — THE SAINTS.

OH, RIGHT, LIKE YOU DIDN'T DO THAT JUST TO BUG ME! DON'T PRETEND YOU'RE BETTER THAN ME BECAUSE YOU'RE NOT!

CHILDREN, CHILDREN! WHY ARE YOU FIGHTING?

SHE'S ALWAYS STARTING TROUBLE! THAT'S NOT VERY CHRISTIAN, IS IT?

HEY! YOU SHOULD TALK!

HMMM... I'M BROTHER MOSES, BY THE WAY. COULD YOU HELP ME FILL THIS BASKET WITH SAND?

YES, BROTHER!

SURE!

BEING A GOOD CHRISTIAN ISN'T EASY, IS IT?

ESPECIALLY FOR SOME PEOPLE!

LIKE WHO?

LIKE ME! I USED TO BE A VIOLENT MAN. I WAS EVEN THE LEADER OF A GANG OF BANDITS.

MY MEN AND I ATTACKED OTHER PEOPLE AND STOLE WHAT WE WANTED.

RUN! IT'S MOSES AND HIS GANG!

ONCE A DOG RUINED MY PLANS FOR A ROBBERY.

I'M LEAVING, BUT I'LL GET REVENGE ON THAT DOG'S OWNER!

I RETURNED LATER TO KILL THAT MAN. JUST BECAUSE HIS DOG BARKED!

I'LL SHOW HIM!

THANK GOD THE MAN WAS NOT HOME WHEN I CAME BACK.

WOW! I'D LIKE TO HEAR MORE ABOUT YOUR LIFE.

UH-OH! THERE'S A HOLE IN YOUR BASKET.

I KNOW.

COME ALONG, CHILDREN. I HAVE TO TAKE THIS BASKET TO A MEETING.

STORM

HOW DID YOU TURN YOUR LIFE AROUND, BROTHER?

ONCE WHEN I WAS ON THE RUN, I STOPPED AT A MONASTERY.

THE BROTHERS TOOK ME IN. THEY DID NOT JUDGE ME FOR MY PAST SINS, BUT SHOWED ME GOD'S LOVE.

I WAS INSPIRED TO BECOME A CHRISTIAN AND A MONK, TOO.

EVERY DAY, I TRY TO BE A GOOD MAN. I'M FAR FROM PERFECT, BUT GOD LOVES ME.

YOU HAVE SINNED, BROTHER. WE ARE GOING TO THINK OF A PUNISHMENT FOR YOU.

I'M SORRY I'M LATE, BROTHERS.

WHAT DO YOU HAVE THERE, BROTHER MOSES?

NOT MUCH!

REALLY!

IT'S A BASKET OF SAND.

BUT IT'S EMPTY. THE SAND LEAKED OUT OF THAT HOLE.

WHY DID YOU BRING SAND TO OUR MEET-ING ANY-WAY?

MY SINS RUN OUT BEHIND ME, LIKE THE SAND. WHO AM I TO JUDGE THE ERRORS OF OTHERS?

HE'S RIGHT. NONE OF US IS PERFECT. WE SHOULD NOT BE JUDGING OUR BROTHER.

PLEASE FORGIVE US.

ONLY GOD CAN JUDGE US. WE MUST FORGIVE EACH OTHER.

THERE'S THE MUSIC!

I'M SORRY I SAID YOU DIDN'T CARE ABOUT YOUR FAITH. I SHOULDN'T HAVE JUDGED YOU LIKE THAT. IT'S NOT LIKE I'M PERFECT.

ME NEITHER! BUT I ALSO JUDGED YOU. I'M SORRY!

IT'S OK. YOU KNOW... SOMETIMES WE DO THAT TO OTHER PEOPLE, TOO.

YEAH... I WISH WE COULD BE MORE LIKE MOSES.

WE CAN! HE MADE A HUGE CHANGE IN HIS LIFE.

SO CAN'T WE MAKE A SMALL CHANGE?

SURE! INSTEAD OF PASSING JUDGEMENT, LET'S BE MORE UNDERSTANDING OF OTHERS.

OKAY! HEY! YOU SHOULD BE... I MEAN... YOU'RE NOT GOING TO WASTE MORE TIME ON... UM...

LATER!

But wait... there's more!

91

"O God, let me know and love you!"

Saint Moses the Black is also known as "the Ethiopian" and "the Desert Christian." His feast day coincides with the August 28, 1963, march on Washington, D.C., by more than 200,000 people seeking civil rights for African-Americans.

Moses was born around the year 330 A.D. We know little about his early life, but he is believed to have been of Ethiopian descent. We do know that he was a slave to the family of an Egyptian official. Strong and violent, Moses eventually escaped from slavery and became the leader of a large gang of bandits. Together they roamed the Nile Valley, robbing and terrorizing households.

After years of this criminal lifestyle, Moses was on the run from the authorities. He came across a group of monks in a monastery in Scete, which was in the desert near Alexandria. Moses was impressed by the dedication of the monks. He admired the peace and contentment of their lives. Eventually their influence led him to give up his wild ways and become a monk himself.

Saint Moses the Black

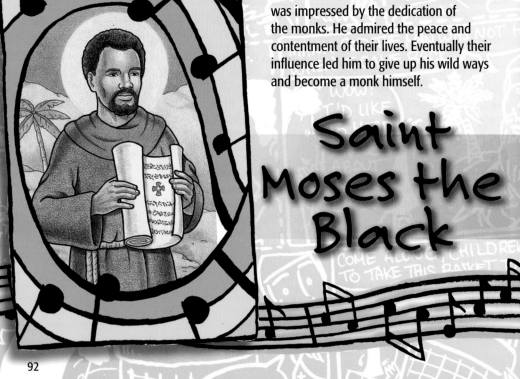

It took a while for Brother Moses to adjust to religious life, though. One night four robbers broke into his hut. To their shock, Moses fought them—and won! He tied them up and dragged them to the chapel, where his fellow monks were at prayer.

"I don't know what to do with them," Moses explained. "It doesn't seem as if it would be Christian to kill them!"

The other monks, of course, agreed. Soon the robbers repented of their sins. They were determined to live better lives. Eventually, because of their admiration for Brother Moses, they all became monks themselves!

Moses was eventually ordained as a priest, which was unusual at that time. He became the spiritual leader of a group of hermits living in the desert. When he was about seventy-five years old, the hermitage was attacked by bandits. Father Moses met the intruders peacefully, but he and the others were all killed. Saint Moses, the former criminal, has become a beloved role model of nonviolence.

Saint Moses was the first black African to be named a saint.

PRAYER

Saint Moses, you show us that no matter how great our sins, Jesus will always forgive us. Help me to be truly sorry for my sins.

Hermits are men or women who live alone or in small communities. They hope to become closer to God through prayer, fasting, sacrifice, and silence. Moses was one of the earliest Desert Fathers of the Scete region in Egypt. These Christian hermits became known for their holiness and wisdom. The spiritual writings of the Desert Fathers are still studied today.

Stepping Stones
The Comic Collection

Written by Diana R. Jenkins
Art by Chris Sabatino

Denver, Chantal, Suki, and Alberto are on a journey—and you can join them! With these fun and inspiring comics, you'll share the ups and downs, problems and joys, successes and failures of a great group of friends. The stepping stones of their lives are leading them on a path toward God.

Won't you follow along? After all, you're on that journey, too!

Paperback
128 pp.
71184
$9.95 ($12.50 Cdn)

Who are the Daughters of St. Paul?

We are Catholic sisters. Our mission is to be like Saint Paul and tell everyone about Jesus! There are so many ways for people to communicate with each other. We want to use all of them so everyone will know how much God loves us. We do this by printing books (you're holding one!), making radio shows, singing, helping people at our bookstores, using the Internet, and in many other ways.

Visit our Web site at www.pauline.org

Pauline
BOOKS & MEDIA

The Daughters of St. Paul operate book and media centers at the following addresses. Visit, call or write the one nearest you today, or find us on the World Wide Web, www.pauline.org

CALIFORNIA
3908 Sepulveda Blvd, Culver City, CA 90230 — 310-397-8676
2640 Broadway Street, Redwood City, CA 94063 — 650-369-4230
5945 Balboa Avenue, San Diego, CA 92111 — 858-565-9181

FLORIDA
145 S.W. 107th Avenue, Miami, FL 33174 — 305-559-6715

HAWAII
1143 Bishop Street, Honolulu, HI 96813 — 808-521-2731
Neighbor Islands call: — 866-521-2731

ILLINOIS
172 North Michigan Avenue, Chicago, IL 60601 — 312-346-4228

LOUISIANA
4403 Veterans Memorial Blvd, Metairie, LA 70006 — 504-887-7631

MASSACHUSETTS
885 Providence Hwy, Dedham, MA 02026 — 781-326-5385

MISSOURI
9804 Watson Road, St. Louis, MO 63126 — 314-965-3512

NEW JERSEY
561 U.S. Route 1, Wick Plaza, Edison, NJ 08817 — 32-572-1200

NEW YORK
64 West 38th Street, New York, NY 10018 — 212-754-1110

PENNSYLVANIA
9171-A Roosevelt Blvd, Philadelphia, PA 19114 — 215-676-9494

SOUTH CAROLINA
243 King Street, Charleston, SC 29401 — 843-577-0175

VIRGINIA
1025 King Street, Alexandria, VA 22314 — 703-549-3806

CANADA
3022 Dufferin Street, Toronto, ON M6B 3T5 — 416-781-9131